TERMS AND CONDITIONS

IMPORTANT - PERMITTED USE AND WARNINGS - READ CAREFULLY BEFORE USING

Licence

Copyright in the software contained in this CD-ROM and in its accompanying material belongs to Scholastic Limited. All rights reserved. © 2007 Scholastic Ltd.

Save for these purposes, or as expressly authorised in the accompanying materials, the software may not be copied, reproduced, used, sold, licensed, transferred, exchanged, hired, or exported in whole or in part or in any manner or form without the prior written consent of Scholastic Ltd. Any such unauthorised use or activities are prohibited and may give rise to civil liabilities and criminal prosecutions.

The material contained on this CD-ROM may only be used in the context for which it was intended in *100 Literacy Framework Lessons*, and is for use only in the school which has purchased the book and CD-ROM, or by the teacher who has purchased the book and CD-ROM. Permission to download images is given for purchasers only and not for users from any lending service. Any further use of the material contravenes Scholastic Ltd's copyright and that of other rights' holders.

This CD-ROM has been tested for viruses at all stages of its production. However, we recommend that you run virus-checking software on your computer systems at all times. Scholastic Ltd cannot accept any responsibility for any loss, disruption or damage to your data or your computer system that may occur as a result of using either the CD-ROM or the data held on it.

YEAR 1

Scottish Primary 1

Minimum specification:
- PC or Mac with a CD-ROM drive and 512 Mb RAM (recommended)
- Windows 98SE or above/Mac OSX.1 or above
- Recommended minimum processor speed: 1 GHz

For all technical support queries, please phone
Scholastic Customer Services on 0845 603 9091

Sylvia Clements, Jean Evans
& Fiona Tomlinson

CREDITS

Authors
Sylvia Clements,
Jean Evans &
Fiona Tomlinson

Commissioning Editor
Fiona Tomlinson

Development Editor
Simret Brar

Project Editor
Rachel Mackinnon

Editor
Kate Element

Assistant Editor
Alex Albrighton

Series Designers
Anna Oliwa &
Joy Monkhouse

Designer
Geraldine Reidy &
Micky Pledge

Book Designer
Q2A Media

Illustrations
Andy Keylock
/ Beehive Illustration

CD-ROM Development
CD-ROM developed in
association with Vivid
Interactive

Narrative © 2007, Jean Evans
Non-fiction © 2007, Fiona Tomlinson
Poetry © 2007, Sylvia Clements
© 2007 Scholastic Ltd

Designed using Adobe InDesign

Published by Scholastic Ltd
Villiers House
Clarendon Avenue
Leamington Spa
Warwickshire CV32 5PR

Visit our website at
www.scholastic.co.uk

Printed by Bell and Bain Ltd
456789 890123456

ACKNOWLEDGEMENTS

The publishers gratefully acknowledge permission to reproduce the following copyright material: **Barefoot Books Ltd** for the use of extracts and illustrations from *Jack and the Beanstalk* by Richard Walker. Text © 1999, Richard Walker, illustrations © 1999, Niamh Sharkey (1999, Barefoot Books). **John Foster** for the use of 'Tastes' and Rosemary Rudd' by John Foster from *Bare Bear and other rhymes* by John Foster © 1999, John Foster (1999, Oxford University Press) and for the use of 'Footprints on the beach' and 'I went to the farm' by John Foster from *My Magic Anorak* by John Foster © 1999, John Foster (1999, Oxford University Press). **Her Majesty's Stationery Office** the use of extracts from *The Primary National Strategy* © Crown copyright, reproduced under the terms of The PSI Licence. **Hodder and Stoughton Ltd** for the use of extracts and illustrations from *The kiss that missed* by David Melling. Text and illustration © 2002, David Melling (2002, Hodder Children's Books) and for the use of an extract and illustration from *Oliver's Vegetables* by Vivian French Text © 1995, Vivian French, Illustration © 1995, Alison Bartlett (1995, Hodder Children's Books). **Frances Lincoln Ltd** for the use of a text extract and illustrations from *Amazing Grace* by Mary Hoffman. Text © 1991, Mary Hoffman, Illustration © 1991, Caroline Binch (1991, Frances Lincoln Ltd). **Macmillan Publishers Ltd** for the use of 'Sniff, sniff, sniff' from *Wriggle and Road! Rhymes to join in with* by Julia Donaldson and Nick Sharratt text © 2004, Julia Donaldson (2004, Macmillan Children's Books). **Mallinson Rendel Publishers Ltd** for the use of an extract and illustrations from *The Other Ark* by Lynley Dodd © 2004, Lynley Dodd (2004, Mallinson Rendel Publishers Ltd). **MBA Literary Agents** on behalf of Gervase Phinn for the use of 'Noises Off' from *What I Like!* by Gervase Phinn © 2005, Gervase Phinn (2005, Child's Play International). **Tony Mitton** for the use of 'Playdough people' by Tony Mitton from *First Verses for the Very Young* chosen by John Foster © 2003, Tony Mitton (2003, Oxford University Press). **Barbara Moore** for the use of 'Soup' by Barbara Moore from *Rhyme Time: Around the Day* compiled by John Foster © 2000, Barbara Moore (2000, Oxford University Press). **Judith Nicholls** for the use of 'Sounds Good' by Judith Nicholls from *Rhyme Time: Around the Day* compiled by John Foster © 2000, Judith Nicholls (2000, Oxford University Press). **The Peters Fraser and Dunlop Group** (www.pfd.co.uk) on behalf of Michael Rosen for the use of 'On the beach' by Michael Rosen and 'Over my toes' by Michael Rosen both from *Tea in the sugar bowl, potato in my shoe* by Michael Rosen © 1987, Michael Rosen (1987, Walker Books Ltd). **The Random House Group Ltd** for the use of text and an illustration from *Fantastic Daisy Artichoke* by Quentin Blake. Text and illustration © 1999, Quentin Blake (1999, Jonathan Cape). **Sally Scott** for the use of 'Dressing up' by Sally Scott from *Themes for Early Years: Myself* by Jean Evans and Lynne Burgess © 2006, Sally Scott (2006, Scholastic Ltd). **Walker Books Ltd** for the use of text extracts and illustrations from *We're going on a bear hunt* by Michael Rosen and illustrated by Helen Oxenbury Text © 1989, Michael Rosen, Illustrations © 1989, Helen Oxenbury (1989, Walker Books Ltd) and an extract and illustration from *We're going on a bear hunt (story play)* replayed by Vivian French and illustrated by Helen Oxenbury based on *We're going on a bear hunt* by Michael Rosen and illustrated by Helen Oxenbury Playscript © 2000, Vivian French Illustrations © 1989, Helen Oxenbury (2000, Walker Books Ltd); for the opening sequence of *We're going on a bear hunt* by Michael Rosen from the book DVD. Illustrations by Helen Oxenbury © 1989, Helen Oxenbury, story © 1989, Michael Rosen read by Emilia Fox and Kevin Whately, music by Lester Barnes (p) and © 2006, Walker Books, produced by King Rollo Films Ltd (2006, Walker Books Ltd); for the use of text extracts and an illustration from "So much" by Trish Cooke. Text © 1994, Trish Cooke. Illustration © 1994, Helen Oxenbury (1994, Walker Books Ltd) and for the use of text extracts and illustrations from *Here come the aliens!* by Colin McNaughton © 1995, Colin McNaughton (1995, Walker Books Ltd). **Celia Warren** for the use of 'Song of the seaside' and 'Sing a song of seasons' by Celia Warren © 2007, Celia Warren (previously unpublished). **West Midland Safari and Leisure Park** for the use of the pictorial map © 2007, West Midland Safari and Leisure Park www.wmsp.co.uk

Every effort has been made to trace copyright holders for the works reproduced in this book, and the publishers apologise for any inadvertent omissions.

British Library Cataloguing-in-Publication Data
A catalogue record for this book is available from the British Library.
ISBN 978-0439-94521-9

CONTENTS

INTRODUCTION
100 Literacy Framework Lessons: Year 1

About the series

The *100 Literacy Framework Lessons* series is a response to the Primary National Strategy's revised Literacy Framework and contains **all new** material. The lessons mirror the structure and learning objectives of the Exemplification Units of the Framework. The CD-ROM provides appropriate and exciting texts and also contains a variety of other resources from videos and images to audio and weblinks, which will help to guide you in implementing the Framework's emphasis on ICT texts. The books and CD-ROMs will be an invaluable resource to help you understand and implement the revised Framework.

The key points of the revised framework are:

- The development of early reading and phonics;
- Coherent and progressive teaching of word-level and sentence-level embedded into learning or taught discretely;
- Following and building upon the teaching sequence from reading to writing and developing comprehension;
- Flexible lessons providing a challenging pace;
- Integration of speaking and listening skills;
- Planning for inclusion;
- Broadening and strengthening pedagogy.

Early reading and phonics

The authors of the *100 Literacy Framework Lessons* have endeavoured to incorporate all of the above with one exception, the teaching of phonics. The Government is advising that phonics is taught using a systematic, discrete and time-limited programme. However, where possible we have made links to phonic focuses that you might want to identify when teaching the lesson.

It is important to note that the renewed Framework is advocating a change from the Searchlight model of teaching early reading to the 'simple view of reading', *"The knowledge and skills within the four Searchlight strategies are subsumed within the two dimensions of word recognition and language*

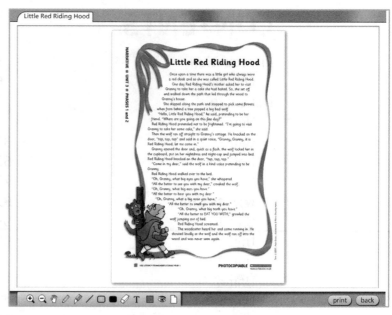

comprehension of the 'two simple views of reading'. For beginner readers, priority should be given to securing word recognition, knowledge and skills" (from the PNS Core Papers document). Phonic work will be time limited and as children develop their early reading skills they will then move from learning to read to learning to learn.

Using the book

The book is divided into three parts, called Blocks: Narrative Block, Non-fiction Block and Poetry Block. This reflects the structure of the renewed Framework planning. The Blocks are divided into Units, each Unit covers a different text-type within the Block, for example in the Narrative Block there might be one Unit which covers 'myths and legends' and another that covers 'plays'. Units are taught on a specified amount of weeks and are split into Phases. Phases vary in length and are essentially a way to focus on a specific part of teaching relating to the Unit. Phases are then divided into days, or lessons, which then contain the teaching activities. Unlike the *100 All New Literacy Hours,* this book has not been divided into terms because one of the main points of the Framework is flexibility and this structure will let teachers adapt to their particular children's needs.

Block [genres] ➤ Units [text-type] ➤ Phases [section of Unit] ➤ Days/Lessons [Individual lessons]

Units

Each Unit covers a different text-type, or genre and because of this each Unit has its own introduction containing the following:

Objectives: All objectives for the Unit are listed under their strand names.

Progression: Statements about the progression that the children should make within the Unit's focus, for example narrative text-type.

Aspects of learning: Key aspects of learning that the Unit covers.

Prior learning: Key elements that the children need to be able to do before they commence the lessons.

Cross-curricular opportunities: Integrating other areas of the curriculum into the literacy lessons.

Resources: Everything required for the lesson that teachers may not have readily available.

Teaching sequence: This is an overview chart of the Unit. It shows the number of Phases, children's objectives, a summary of activities and the learning outcomes.

Unit lesson plans

The lesson plans all follow the same format. There are three columns and each contains different information.

Key features: The key features column provides an at-a-glance view of the key aspects of learning covered in the lesson.

Stages: The stages column provides the main lesson plans.

Additional opportunities: This column provides additional opportunities for the lesson. This is where there will be links made to phonics, high frequency words, support or extension activities and any other relevant learning opportunities.

End of Phase

At the end of each Phase there are three boxes containing Guided reading or writing ideas, Assessment ideas and Further work.

Guided: The guided box contains ideas for guided reading or writing. These have been included separately as there seems to be a trend to do this work outside of the literacy hour lesson. These ideas can either be integrated into a lesson or taught at a separate time.

Assessment: There are two types of assessment.

End of Phase assessments: These are mainly observations of the children or simple tasks to see whether they have understood what has been taught in the Phase. Teachers are referred back to the learning outcomes in the teaching sequence in the Unit introduction.

End of Unit assessments: These are activities which range from interactive activities, to working from a stimulus image, to completing a photocopiable sheet. They can be found on the CD-ROM accompanying this series.

Further work: Further work provides opportunities for the teacher to extend or support the children following the assessment activity.

Photocopiable pages

At the end of each Unit are the photocopiable pages. These can also be found on the CD-ROM.

Using the CD-ROM

This is a basic guide for using the CD-ROM; for more detailed information please go to 'How to use the CD-ROM' on the start-up screen of the CD-ROM.

The CD-ROM contains resources for each book in the series. These might include: text extracts, differentiated text extracts, editable text extracts, photocopiable pages, interactive activities, images, videos, audio files, PowerPoint files, weblinks and assessment activities. There are also skeleton frames based on Sue Palmer's skeletons for teaching non-fiction text types. Also on the CD-ROM are the lesson notes for easy planning as Word file documents.

You can access resources in a number of ways:

Phase menu: The Phase menu provides all the resources used in that Phase. There are tabs at the top of the page denoting the resource type, for example 'Text'. If you click on this tab you will see a series of buttons to your left; if you press these then you will be taken to the other texts used within that Phase. You can print two versions of the text: either the screen – which shows any annotations made (see Whiteboard tools below) or Print PDF version, which will print an A4 size.

Resources menu: The resource menu lists every resource that is available on the CD-ROM. You can search by type of resource.

Fairy tale castle

Whiteboard tools: This series contains a set of whiteboard tools. These can be used with any interactive whiteboard and from a computer connected to a projector. The tools available are: Hand tool – so that when you zoom in you can move around the screen; Zoom in; Zoom out; Pen tool for freehand writing or drawing; Highlighter; Line tool; Box tool; Text tool; Eraser tool; Clear screen; Hide annotations; Colour. You cannot save any changes made to the texts so always remember to 'Print Screen' when you annotate the CD-ROM pages.

Speak and listen for a range of purposes on paper and on screen strand checklist

	Narrative Unit 1	Narrative Unit 2	Narrative Unit 3	Narrative Unit 4	Non-fiction Unit 1	Non-fiction Unit 2	Non-fiction Unit 3	Non-fiction Unit 4	Non-fiction Unit 5	Poetry Unit 1	Poetry Unit 2	Poetry Unit 3
Strand 1 Speaking												
Tell stories and describe incidents from their own experience in an audible voice.	✔		✔		✔	✔	✔		✔			
Retell stories, ordering events using story language.	✔		✔									
Interpret a text by reading aloud with some variety in pace and emphasis.		✔								✔	✔	✔
Experiment with and build new stores of words to communicate in different contexts.												
Strand 2 Listening and responding												
Listen with sustained concentration, building new stores of words in different contexts.	✔	✔	✔		✔	✔	✔	✔		✔	✔	✔
Listen to and follow instructions accurately, asking for help and clarification if necessary.					✔	✔		✔				
Listen to tapes or video and express views about how a story or information has been presented.			✔									
Strand 3 Group discussion and interaction												
Take turns to speak, listen to others' suggestions and talk about what they are going to do.		✔	✔		✔	✔						
Ask and answer questions, make relevant contributions, offer suggestions and take turns.					✔	✔	✔	✔		✔	✔	✔
Explain their views to others in a small group; decide how to report the group's views to the class.		✔							✔	✔	✔	✔
Strand 4 Drama												
Explore familiar themes and characters through improvisation and role play.	✔		✔	✔								
Act out own and well-known stories, using voices for characters.			✔									
Discuss why they like a performance.												

Read for a range of purposes on paper and on screen strand checklist

	Narrative Unit 1	Narrative Unit 2	Narrative Unit 3	Narrative Unit 4	Non-fiction Unit 1	Non-fiction Unit 2	Non-fiction Unit 3	Non-fiction Unit 4	Non-fiction Unit 5	Poetry Unit 1	Poetry Unit 2	Poetry Unit 3
Strand 5 Word recognition												
Recognise and use alternative ways of pronouncing the graphemes already taught.					✔	✔	✔	✔	✔	✔	✔	✔
Recognise and use alternative ways of spelling the graphemes already taught.					✔	✔	✔	✔	✔	✔	✔	✔
Identify the constituent parts of two-and-three-syllable words to support application of phonic knowledge and skills.					✔	✔	✔	✔	✔		✔	✔
Recognise automatically an increasing number of familiar high frequency words.					✔	✔	✔	✔	✔		✔	✔
Apply phonic knowledge and skills as the prime approach to reading and spelling unfamiliar words which are not completely decodable.	✔	✔	✔	✔	✔	✔	✔	✔	✔	✔	✔	✔
Read more challenging texts which can be decoded using their acquired phonic knowledge and skills, along with automatic recognition of high frequency words.				✔	✔	✔	✔	✔	✔		✔	✔
Read and spell phonically decodable two-and-three-syllable words.				✔	✔	✔		✔	✔		✔	✔
Strand 6 Word structure and spelling												
Spell new words using phonics as the prime approach.	✔	✔		✔	✔		✔	✔	✔	✔	✔	✔
Segment sounds into their constituent phonemes in order to spell them correctly.	✔			✔	✔	✔	✔	✔	✔	✔	✔	✔
Recognise and use alternative ways of spelling the graphemes already taught.	✔			✔	✔	✔	✔	✔	✔		✔	✔
Use knowledge of common inflections in spelling such as plurals, -ly, -er.				✔	✔	✔	✔	✔	✔		✔	✔
Read and spell phonically decodable two-and-three-syllable words.				✔	✔		✔	✔	✔		✔	✔
Strand 7 Understanding and interpreting texts												
Identify the main events and characters in stories, and find specific information in simple texts.	✔	✔	✔		✔	✔	✔		✔			
Use syntax and context when reading for meaning.	✔	✔		✔								
Make predictions showing an understanding of ideas, events and characters.			✔					✔				
Recognise the main elements that shape different texts.			✔	✔		✔	✔	✔	✔			
Explore the effect of patterns of language and repeated words and phrases.		✔			✔					✔	✔	✔
Strand 8 Engaging with and responding to texts												
Select books for personal reading and give reasons for choices.	✔	✔	✔					✔				
Visualise and comment on events, characters and ideas, making imaginative links to own experiences.	✔		✔				✔			✔	✔	✔
Distinguish fiction and non-fiction texts and the different purposes for reading them.					✔	✔						

Write for a range of purposes on paper and on screen strand checklist	Narrative Unit 1	Narrative Unit 2	Narrative Unit 3	Narrative Unit 4	Non-fiction Unit 1	Non-fiction Unit 2	Non-fiction Unit 3	Non-fiction Unit 4	Non-fiction Unit 5	Poetry Unit 1	Poetry Unit 2	Poetry Unit 3
Strand 9 Creating and shaping texts												
Independently choose what to write about, plan and follow it through.	✔	✔	✔		✔	✔	✔	✔				
Use key features of narrative in their own writing.	✔	✔	✔	✔								
Convey information and ideas in simple non-narrative forms.					✔	✔	✔	✔	✔			
Find and use new and interesting words and phrases, including story language.		✔	✔					✔		✔	✔	✔
Create short simple texts on paper and on screen which combine words with images (and sounds).	✔		✔	✔	✔	✔	✔	✔	✔	✔	✔	✔
Strand 10 Text structure and organisation												
Write chronological and non-chronological texts using simple structures.	✔	✔			✔		✔	✔	✔			
Group written sentences together in chunks of meaning or subject.			✔		✔	✔	✔	✔				
Strand 11 Sentence structure and punctuation												
Compose and write simple sentences independently to communicate meaning.	✔	✔	✔	✔	✔	✔	✔	✔	✔			
Use capital letters and full stops when punctuating simple sentences.		✔	✔	✔	✔	✔	✔	✔				
Strand 12 Presentation												
Write most letters, correctly formed and orientated, using a comfortable and efficient pencil grip.		✔						✔		✔	✔	✔
Write with spaces between words accurately.								✔		✔	✔	✔
Use the space bar and keyboard to type name and simple text.			✔	✔	✔	✔	✔		✔	✔		

NARRATIVE
UNIT 1 Stories with familiar settings

Speak and listen for range of purposes on paper and on screen

Strand 1 Speaking
■ Tell stories and incidents from their own experience in an audible voice.
■ Retell stories, ordering events using story language.
Strand 2 Listening and responding
■ Listen with sustained concentration, building new stores of words in different contexts.
Strand 4 Drama
■ Explore familiar themes and characters through improvisation and role play.

Read for a range of purposes on paper and on screen

Strand 5 Word recognition: decoding (reading) and encoding (spelling)
■ Apply phonic knowledge and skills as the prime approach to reading and spelling unfamiliar words that are not completely decodable.
Strand 6 Word structure and spelling
■ Spell new words using phonics as the prime approach.
■ Segment sounds into their constituent phonemes in order to spell them.
■ Recognise and use alternative ways of spelling the graphemes already taught.
Strand 7 Understanding and interpreting texts
■ Identify the main events and characters in stories, and find specific information in simple texts.
■ Use syntax and context when reading for meaning.
Strand 8 Engaging and responding to texts
■ Select books for personal reading and give reasons for choices.
■ Visualise and comment on events, characters and ideas, making imaginative links to own experiences.

Write for a range of purposes on paper and on screen

Strand 9 Creating and shaping texts
■ Independently choose what to write about, plan and follow it through.
■ Use key features of narrative in their own writing.
■ Create short simple texts on paper and on screen which combine words with images (and sounds).
Strand 10 Text structure and organisation
■ Write chronological and non-chronological texts using simple structures.
Strand 11 Sentence structure and punctuation
■ Compose and write simple sentences independently to communicate meaning.

Progression in narrative

In this year children are moving towards:
■ Listening to and reading a range of stories on page and screen which provoke different responses; identifying the beginning, middle and end in stories and recalling the main events; recognising main characters and settings using evidence from illustration and text.
■ Creating stories orally, on page and screen, that will impact on listeners and readers in a range of ways; using patterns and language from familiar stories in own writing.

▶

UNIT 1 ◄ Stories with familiar settings *continued*

Key aspects of learning covered in this Unit

Creative thinking
Children will apply imaginative ideas to create ideas for drama and story writing based on familiar incidents and settings.

Motivation
Children will have a clear goal for their independent writing – composing three complete sentences – and will be able to assess their own progress in achieving that goal as they read through what they have written.

Evaluation
Children will discuss success criteria for their written work, give feedback to others and begin to judge the effectiveness of their own writing.

Social skills
When developing collaborative writing children will learn about listening to and respecting other people's ideas.

Communication
Children will develop their ability to discuss as they work collaboratively in paired, group and whole-class contexts. They will communicate outcomes orally, in writing and through ICT if appropriate.

Prior learning

Before starting this Unit check that the children can:
■ Listen attentively to stories and identify the main characters and setting.
■ Re-enact a story they have heard and include the main character and some of the main events.
■ Begin to form simple sentences.
If they need further support refer to a prior Unit or to the Foundation Stage.

Resources

Sequence 1, Phase 1: *Oliver's Vegetables* by Vivian French (Hodder); *Oliver's Vegetables* extract ❦; Photocopiable page 26 'Oliver's vegetables'; *What Shall We Do, Blue Kangaroo?* by Emma Chichester Clark (Collins); *The Good Mood Hunt* by Hiawyn Oram (OUP)

Sequence 1, Phase 2: Photocopiable page 26 'Oliver's vegetables'; Models of vegetables; Days of the week cards; Dressing-up clothes; Photocopiable page 27 'Storybook characters'

Sequence 1, Phase 3: *Oliver's Vegetables* by Vivian French (Hodder); *Oliver's Vegetables* extract ❦; Photocopiable page 28 'The growing sequence of a pea'; Boots, dressing-up clothes and garden-related props; Interactive activity 'Vegetable garden' ❦; Photocopiable page 29 'The gardener's diary'; A growing story

Sequence 2, Phase 1: *Amazing Grace* by Mary Hoffman (Frances Lincoln); *Amazing Grace – extracts 1* and *2* ❦; Picture of a ballet dancer; Popular ballet music; A ballet tutu; The traditional tale 'Anansi the spider'; *Helpful Henry* by Ruth Brown (Andersen Press); *Harry's Box* by Angela McAllister (Bloomsbury)

Sequence 2, Phase 2: *Amazing Grace – extract 2* by Mary Hoffman ❦; Dressing-up clothes and props for storybook characters; A familiar story

Sequence 2, Phase 3: *Amazing Grace* by Mary Hoffman (Frances Lincoln); Photocopiable page 30 'Character, setting, event'; *Dressing up* by Sally Scott ❦; Photocopiable page 29 'The Gardener's diary'; A prepared worksheet showing three boxes with space around them; Assessment activity 'Story structure' ❦

Cross-curricular opportunities

Family (familiar events at home, family members)

UNIT 1 ■ Teaching sequence 1

Phase	Children's objectives	Summary of activities	Learning outcomes
1	I can listen to a story and respond with memories. I can listen and respond to stories. I can compare stories.	Choose a favourite character from memory to draw and write about. Retell *Oliver's Vegetables* in sequence and make a book about it. Invent two characters for a story and write about them.	Children can identify the main character and setting in a story using evidence from the illustrations and text.
2	I can re-enact a story. I can retell a story.	Use props to support sequencing and re-enact *Oliver's Vegetables*. Use stick puppets to retell *Oliver's Vegetables*.	Children can re-enact a story, sequencing the main events and using phrases from the text.
3	I can tell a story based on a personal experience. I can talk about writing. I can create a storyboard. I can write a story with three sentences.	Make up a story about a familiar garden, drawing characters and writing words to describe them. Dramatise the planned story and observe sentence writing. Use photographs to plan the story and write sentences about them Create a simple storyboard. Write a three-page storybook.	Children can write three simple sentences to tell a story.

UNIT 1 ■ Teaching sequence 2

Phase	Children's objectives	Summary of activities	Learning outcomes
1	I can listen and talk about a story. I can listen to stories and link them to my own experiences. I can compare stories and decide a favourite.	Tell stories about past memories. Decide which story character they would like to be. Write two sentences about imaginary adult and child characters.	Children can identify the main character and setting in a story using evidence from the illustrations and text.
2	I can re-enact a story. I can retell a story.	Re-enact the story of *Amazing Grace* after listing the characters involved. Retell the story of *Amazing Grace* using lists created on Day 1 as prompts.	Children can re-enact a story, sequencing the main events and using phrases from the text.
3	I can tell a story based on a personal experience. I can observe an adult modelling sentence writing. I can talk about writing. I can create a storyboard. I can write a story with three sentences.	Make up and tell a story based on experiences of dressing up. Read a poem about dressing up to stimulate ideas for story dramatisation. Use photographs of Day 2 to plan the story and write sentences about them. Create a simple storyboard. Write a three-page storybook.	Children can write three simple sentences to tell a story.

Provide copies of the objectives for the children.

DAY 1 ■ Respond to a story with memories

Key features	Stages	Additional opportunities
	Introduction Read the story *Oliver's Vegetables* to the class. Ask: *Who is the story about? What happens in the story?* Use and explain the terms *setting, main character* and *events*. Invite them to retell the story, using words such as *first, next, at the end*.	**Phonics:** m*i*ss, b*u*s, best, r*a*n, g*o*t, b*i*g, h*a*d, c*a*n, c*u*t **HFW:** days of the week
Social skills: turn taking	**Speaking and listening** Display the *Oliver's Vegetables* extract from the CD-ROM, showing Oliver's Gran and Grandpa in their garden. Remind the children how Oliver enjoyed visiting them and finding vegetables growing in the garden. Discuss the children's experiences of visiting grandparents or other relatives. Divide the class into pairs to talk about these memories and describe someone they enjoy visiting. Explain that they will be reporting their memories back to the class. Bring the class together and ask pairs to take turns to tell the class about their partner's chosen character. Stimulate responses to each other's memories by asking questions such as: *Why have you chosen this character? What is special about him/her?*	**Support:** encourage use of phonics when writing under pictures
Creative thinking: applying imaginative ideas	**Independent work** Invite the children to draw a picture of their chosen character and ask them to write something about them underneath. ✻ **Plenary** Bring the class together and look at the children's drawings. Re-read *Oliver's Vegetables* or the extract from the CD-ROM. Discuss the story using the words *character, setting,* and *event*.	**Extend:** introduce more imaginative vocabulary to support descriptions of characters from the children's memories

DAY 2 ■ Listen and respond to stories

Key features	Stages	Additional opportunities
	Introduction Ask the children to recall the story they heard the day before, encouraging them to comment on characters, settings and events.	**Phonics:** m*u*m, b*u*s, r*a*n, b*u*t, b*i*g, c*a*n, c*u*t, s*a*t **HFW:** days of the week
Communication: discussing their work collaboratively	**Speaking and listening** Display the *Oliver's Vegetables* extract from the CD-ROM. Ask: *What part does Grandpa's garden play in the story?* Work together on retelling the story. Divide the class into small groups and supply each group with cut out pictures from photocopiable page 26 'Oliver's vegetables'. Ask them to arrange the pictures in order to remind them of the story sequence. Bring the class back together to compare their sequences. Retell the story using one of them.	**Extend:** recall the names of all the vegetables without the prompt cards
Creative thinking: applying imaginative ideas	**Independent work** Provide each child with a copy of the photocopiable sheet. Ask them to cut out the pictures, colour them, arrange them in order and stick them to a strip of paper folded eight times to form a zig-zag book. Encourage them to write the names of the vegetables under the relevant pictures in their books. **Plenary** Bring the children back together and invite them to point to pages in their books to represent what happened first, next and at the end of the story.	**Support:** encourage reference to days of the week list when writing

DAY 3 Compare stories

Key features	Stages	Additional opportunities
	## Introduction Read two stories such as *What Shall We Do Blue Kangaroo?* and *The Good Mood Hunt* and compare characters, settings and events. Remind children of the story of *Oliver's Vegetables* told earlier. Which of the three stories did they like best?	**Phonics:** dog, cat, wet, ran, bed **HFW:** one, two, three, four, five
Social skills: turn taking, listening and respecting ideas	## Speaking and listening Explain that you are going to read one of these three stories again. Ask each child to choose a favourite one and give a reason for this choice. Read the most popular story again and ask the children if they notice anything new in the words or illustrations. Read the next most popular story and discuss characters, settings and events. Make a list of the characters in all three stories under the headings *Adults* and *Children*. Ask which adults would be most fun to be with and why. Ask questions about the child characters, for example: *Which ones are happiest? Who would make the best friend?*	
Creative thinking: ideas based on own experiences	## Independent work Ask the children to think of two characters for a story – an adult and a child. Invite them to draw pictures of their chosen characters and think of up to ten words to describe each one. Can they suggest an event that happens between them?	**Support:** encourage use of phonics when writing words **Extend:** make a list of words to describe a chosen character from each of the stories
	## Plenary Bring the class together and choose children to introduce their characters and describe them. Are there any animals or fantasy creatures?	

Guided reading
Find pages in the featured stories that have a high number of CVC words. Ask children to find the words. What do the children notice about pairs of words such as *hat* and *cat*, *dad* and *lad*?
Read *Oliver's Vegetables* and ask the children to point to the days of the week.

Assessment
Can the children write three simple sentences about the characters they recall or imagine?
Can they describe different story settings?
Refer back to the learning outcomes on page 11.

Further work
Encourage children who need support to write one sentence about a character and setting.
Extend children by asking them to develop their sentences to create a story with a definite beginning, middle and end based on the imaginary characters created on Day 3.

Drama

DAY 1 ■ Re-enacting stories

Key features	Stages	Additional opportunities
	Introduction Ask the children to recall the story of *Oliver's Vegetables* and write a list of the vegetables grown by Oliver's Grandpa on a large sheet of paper. Now display photocopiable page 26 'Oliver's vegetables' and tick the ones that the children have mentioned. Have they forgotten any?	**Phonics:** spina*ch*, *ch*ips, fini*sh*, lun*ch* **HFW:** can't, don't
Creative thinking: applying imaginative ideas for drama **Communication:** working collaboratively	**Speaking and listening** Explain that you would like the children to help you to re-enact the story of *Oliver's Vegetables*. Say that the words do not need to be exactly the same but should follow the main events. Tell them that remembering the days of the week and the order in which Oliver picked the vegetables might help with this. Put the children into groups of four and ask them to choose who will play the parts of Oliver, Mum, Grandpa and Gran. Provide plastic or papier-mâché model vegetables and days of the week cards. Ask the children to arrange them in sequence as they appear in the story, with a vegetable next to each card. Encourage children to use this sequence to structure their re-enactment, creating their own dialogue as they go.	**Support:** talk about the story sequence as they work **Extend:** invent more extensive dialogue between the characters
	Independent work Ask children to consider how their characters will look and how their voices will sound. You could supply dressing-up clothes for them to get into role.	
	Plenary Choose a group to re-enact the story and discuss how it could be developed.	

DAY 2 ■ Retelling stories

Key features	Stages	Additional opportunities
	Introduction Ask the children to recall times when someone has told them a story. What did they enjoy about the experience? Explain that you would like them to become storytellers, telling one another the story of *Oliver's Vegetables*.	**Phonics:** be*st*, la*st* **HFW:** days of the week
Social skills: listening to others and taking turns **Communication:** working collaboratively and sharing ideas as a whole group	**Speaking and listening** Talk about the idea of retelling a story. Emphasise the important things the children need to remember, such as characters, settings and events. Write the days of the week on the board and read them together. Ask the children how remembering the order of the days will help them to retell the story. Put the children into pairs and provide each pair with an enlarged copy of photocopiable page 27 'Storybook characters' to cut out, colour and stick to lollipop sticks. Encourage the children to take turns to tell the story to one another, using the character puppets to help them. Suggest that they tell the story twice, so that they can modify or develop it after listening to their partner's version. Bring the class together to discuss their storytelling skills.	**Support:** provide story prompts if necessary **Extend:** individual children tell the story to a small group of children
Creative thinking: applying their imaginative ideas	**Independent work** Ask the children to draw a picture of an event in the story and write a sentence about it. Encourage them to think about what happens before and after the event. Let them show each other their work and talk about their chosen event.	
	Plenary Bring the class together and ask them to help you to retell a different story.	

Guided reading

Read *Oliver's Vegetables* and concentrate on the double consonant combinations *ch* and *sh* to help children to read the words *spinach, chips, finish, lunch*. Find and read more words with these combinations in other books.

Read *Oliver's Vegetables* and focus on the HFW *can't* and *don't*. Explain the purpose of the apostrophe. Make up sentences using these words.

Assessment

Can the children work in groups of four to re-enact a story and sequence the main events?
Refer back to the learning outcomes on page 11.

Further work

Encourage children who need support to choose one event from the story, at the beginning, middle or end, to re-enact. Extend children by asking them to invent voices and create dialogue for the characters in their story.

DAY 1 ■ Telling stories based on personal experience

Key features	Stages	Additional opportunities
Social skills: sharing experiences and listen to one another's stories	**Introduction** Ask the children what they remember about the stories they read in the previous five lessons. Did they identify with the experiences of any of the characters, for example, being in a bad mood like Hannah? Encourage them to tell stories based on these experiences.	**Phonics:** *shed, seed, can, plant* **Support:** tell the experience as they remember it
Communication: discussing experiences and ideas as a whole class and in pairs	**Speaking and listening** Read *Oliver's Vegetables* and discuss how Oliver visits his grandparents' house daily. Discuss the children's experiences of visiting relatives. Do any of them help in a garden? What do they do? What is growing there? Explain that you are going to ask the children to think of a story about a garden they know. Display the *Oliver's Vegetables* extract from the CD-ROM to stimulate ideas for characters for their story and garden related objects they might mention. Compile a class list of possible ideas for characters and events and keep a copy. Put the children into pairs to decide upon a story idea together. Bring the children together and ask pairs to talk about their story idea.	**Extend:** use story language such as *A long time ago* and *at the end*
Creative thinking: using imaginative ideas to support future drama and story writing	**Independent work** Leave the *Oliver's Vegetables* extract on display and invite the children to draw pictures of their garden as they imagine it will look in their story. Encourage them to name characters and label some of the objects on the drawing.	
	Plenary Bring the children together and ask some pairs to tell their stories.	

DAY 2 ■ Modelling the writing

Key features	Stages	Additional opportunities
	Introduction Display the *Oliver's Vegetables* extract from the CD-ROM, and the characters and event list, to remind the children of the story ideas they had the day before. Explain that they are going to start writing down these ideas as stories.	**Phonics:** *shed, seed, can, plant* **HFW:** children read words *first, next, last*
Creative thinking: applying imaginative ideas for drama and story writing	**Speaking and listening** Talk together about possible story themes, emphasising the importance of the changing seasons in a garden. Display photocopiable page 28 'The growing sequence of a pea' and decide together upon the correct sequence introducing the words *first, next* and *last*. Divide the class into groups of four and provide each group with a small selection of suitable boots, dressing-up clothes and garden related resources to use as props. Encourage the children to use the props fully to dramatise their stories, taking four photographs of each group at various stages of development.	**Extend:** encourage more adventurous vocabulary to add excitement to the story
	Independent work While the other children are engaged in dramatisation, invite groups to take turns to create their own gardens using the interactive activity 'Vegetable garden'. Explain that this will help them to imagine the story garden.	
	Plenary Bring the children together and discuss how the stories are developing. Show one of the photographs you have taken and demonstrate how to write a sentence about it. Explain that they will be using their photographs and sequencing sheets the next day to plan out their stories in more detail.	

DAY 3 ■ Talking for writing

Key features	Stages	Additional opportunities
	Introduction Remind the children of the story they created in their groups the day before and show them some of the photographs you have taken. Explain that they are going to use these photographs as a simple story plan.	**HFW:** first, next, last
Social skills: listening and respecting ideas through collaboration **Evaluation:** giving feedback to others and judging their own writing	**Speaking and listening** Choose three photographs depicting one of the groups and display these one by one to demonstrate the beginning, middle and end of the story. Encourage the children in this group to tell everybody what is happening in each photo. Demonstrate how to write a simple sentence about each photograph. Say each sentence aloud and ask the children to do the same. Modify it if necessary until they are they satisfied with the final version. Ask the children to go into the same groups again and give them printed copies of their photographs. Invite them to arrange the photographs in order and take turns to make up sentences to tell the story.	**Support:** model sentence punctuation
	Independent work Ask the children to take one photograph at a time and decide in their groups on the best sentence to write about it. Working together, ask them to put the photographs in order, write their sentences and read the story.	
	Plenary Invite groups to take turns to hold up a photograph each and read the corresponding sentence. Discuss the finished stories.	

DAY 4 ■ Storyboarding

Key features	Stages	Additional opportunities
	Introduction Invite groups of children who did not share their stories the day before to do so. Discuss the experience of creating a story. Were the photographs helpful? Explain the idea of using a storyboard to plan out the sequence of events.	**HFW:** days of the week
Social skills: turn taking and sharing **Communication:** collaborative exchange of ideas	**Speaking and listening** Tell the children that they are going to use a type of storyboard to plan a story about gardens. Display photocopiable page 29 'The gardener's diary' and explain that this shows three boxes in a diary for a gardener to write about events that have happened. Can they think how they could use this page to plan out the events in a story? Read a 'growing' story such as *Billy's Sunflower* or *The Tiny Seed*. Emphasise the order of events. Put the children into pairs and provide each pair with a photocopiable sheet. Invite them to make up a similar story that takes place in a garden over a period of time. Suggest that they draw pictures and write sentences depicting what happens at the beginning, middle and end.	**Support:** write a few relevant words rather than a sentence **Extend:** create different storyboards on popular themes
Evaluation: discussing criteria for written work	**Independent work** Ask pairs of children to read their storyboard to each other, telling the story depicted using phrases such as *At the beginning..., and then..., at the end...* After listening, decide on any modifications to produce a final version. Invite the children to decorate the border with tools, flowers, vegetable and fruits.	
	Plenary Bring the children back together to share their diary pages.	

DAY 5 ■ Writing the story

Key features	Stages	Additional opportunities
	Introduction Talk about the stories the children have planned and written during the week on the themes of families, homes and gardens. Explain that these are the easiest stories to write because they are about things that the children know a lot about.	
Social skills: listening to and commenting on partner's ideas	**Speaking and listening** Tell the children that today they are going to use their storyboards from the day before to make up a storybook all by themselves. Put the children into pairs and supply them with their storyboards. Encourage discussion between the two children in each pair about the story they have planned.	
Creative thinking: applying imaginative ideas based on familiar events **Evaluation:** giving feedback and beginning to judge the effectiveness of their writing	**Independent work** Provide each child with three sheets of paper to form pages representing the beginning, middle and end of the story. Invite them to compose their pages using the storyboard information, including an illustration and simple sentence on each page. Ask them to say their sentences before writing them and then keep re-reading what they have written to check for meaning and accuracy. Once they have completed the pages ask them to discuss them with their partner to judge the effectiveness of their writing. Is it clear how the story starts, what happens next and how the story ends?	**Support:** segment sounds to write unfamiliar words **Extend:** add additional pages to develop the story
Social skills: sharing ideas	**Plenary** Bring the children back together and invite them to read some of their stories to the others. Make the finished stories into a class book to read through together.	

Guided writing

Ask children to rehearse sentences orally before writing them down. Concentrate on correct sentence punctuation. Encourage children to segment sounds to write unfamiliar words.

Assessment

Can the children make a story linked to a familiar setting and write three sentences to depict the sequence of their story beginning, middle and end? Ask the children to write three simple sentences to tell a story. Refer back to the learning outcomes on page 11.

Further work

Let children who need support draw a picture about a single event they remember and help them to write a simple sentence about it. Support those who need extra practice with correct letter formation.
To extend children, ask them to write additional sentences on each page to add detail.

DAY 1 ■ Talking about stories

Key features	Stages	Additional opportunities
	Introduction Display *Amazing Grace – extract 1* from the CD-ROM, showing Grace and her Nana. Ask the children if they know the story the picture comes from, and explain the context briefly if they are unfamiliar with it. Can they think why the main character is called Amazing Grace? Read the story, identifying settings, main character and events, and focusing on *first*, *next*, *at the end*.	**Phonics:** *act*, *web*, *hid*, peg-leg, *cat*, *sad* **HFW:** Saturday
Social skills: turn taking	**Speaking and listening** Recall how Grace enjoyed listening to stories from Nana's long memory. Display *Amazing Grace – extract 2* from the CD-ROM showing Grace sharing a story with her dolls. Read the words to find out other ways that Grace enjoyed stories. Do the children make up stories, have stories read to them from books, or watch TV, film or video versions? Which of these ways of hearing stories do they enjoy most? Divide the class into pairs and say that you would like them to talk to their partners about their favourite way of hearing a story.	**Support:** focus on describing the character and not the events
Social skills: sharing experiences	**Independent work** Invite children to draw a picture of themselves listening to or watching their story in their favourite way, perhaps going to the cinema or watching TV. Ask them to write a sentence underneath it.	**Extend:** use more imaginative vocabulary to describe responses to ballet music and dancing
	Plenary Bring the class together, share the children's drawings and read out some of their sentences. What is the most popular way of hearing stories?	

DAY 2 ■ Listening to stories and linking to own experiences

Key features	Stages	Additional opportunities
	Introduction Read the story of *Amazing Grace*, looking closely at illustrations and re-reading words to identify characters, settings and events. Ask questions about events leading to the conclusion. Why did Grace think she couldn't be Peter Pan? What happened at her audition? How did the story end?	**Phonics:** *lad*, *tub*, *mum*, *dad*, *hat*, *cat* **HFW:** school
Social skills: sharing experiences and listening to others	**Speaking and listening** Show the children a ballet dancer picture and play some popular ballet music. Did the children like the music? Have they ever been to a theatre? Look at the pictures of Grace and Nana going to the ballet. What did Grace do afterwards? Pass around a tutu and talk about clothes the children like to dress up in. Ask pairs of children to tell each other about a storybook character they would like to be. Explain that they will be reporting this back to the class. Bring the class together and have children tell one another about their partner's character and the part they play in the story.	**Support:** ask simplified questions and refer to pictures for clues
	Independent work Invite children to draw a picture of their character taking part in an event from the story and write a sentence about what is happening.	
	Plenary Read one of Grace's favourite stories, 'Anansi the Spider', and identify the characters, settings and events.	

DAY 3 ■ Choosing a favourite story

Key features	Stages	Additional opportunities
	Introduction Read two stories such as *Helpful Henry* and *Harry's Box* and compare the characters, settings and events. Remind children of the stories read earlier and vote on which one to read again.	
	Speaking and listening Read the most popular story and ask the children if they notice anything new in the words or illustrations when hearing it a second time. Now read the next most popular story and discuss characters, settings and events. Put the children into four groups and give each group one of the storybooks and a large sheet of paper. Ask them to write the name of the main character at the top of the paper and then the names of any family members who are mentioned in the story. How do the adults react to the main character's actions? Are they happy, sad, cross, worried, amused, pleased or helpful?	**Extend:** write two or three words to describe each character on the list
Evaluation: judging success criteria for written work; giving feedback to others and judging the effectiveness of their own writing	**Independent work** Ask the children to think of two characters for a story – an adult and a child. Invite them to draw pictures of their characters and think of a sentence about each one. Can they suggest an event that happens between them?	**Support:** encourage use of phonics when writing words
	Plenary Bring the class together and choose children to introduce their characters and read their sentences. Discuss the words chosen to describe the characters and the event. Do the children think that their sentences could be improved?	**Support:** encourage use of phonics when reading words

Guided reading
Encourage children to read words in Henry's Box by segmenting sounds into constituent phonemes such as *when*, *took*, *ship*, *bone*.
Find rhyming words in *Helpful Henry* such as *woke* and *soak*, *passed* and *fast*, and discuss how different graphemes can create the same phoneme.

Assessment
Can the children identify the main character and setting in a story using evidence from the illustrations and text?
Refer back to the learning outcomes on page 11.

Further work
Offer children who need support help with sentence structure and punctuation.
Extend children by asking them to write a detailed sentence about the main character or setting from their favourite story.

DAY 1 ▪ Re-enacting the story

Key features	Stages	Additional opportunities
	Introduction Ask the children to recall the story of *Amazing Grace*. Display *Amazing Grace – extract 2* from the CD-ROM, showing Grace and her dolls and help them to read the text aloud, emphasising HFW and using phonics as the prime approach to reading new and familiar words. Explain that you would like the children to help you to re-enact Grace's story.	**Phonics:** *up, if, in, from, on, just, and, had, act* **HFW:** *girl, were, her, or, from, out, would, them*
Creative thinking: applying imaginative ideas for drama	**Speaking and listening** Ask the children to recall the main characters in the story, and those that Grace dressed up as, write them alongside the picture and keep a copy. Demonstrate how to use the book to help with the spelling of names and then read them again. Rearrange the names until the children are satisfied that they are in the correct order. Divide the children into two groups to re-enact the story. Suggest they use the list they have made to decide on the parts they will play. Provide a good selection of dressing-up clothes and props for each group. Encourage children to structure their dramatisation on the sequence of events and then create their own dialogue as they go along. Suggest that they might need a narrator.	**Support:** encourage children to look at a picture of Grace in character to help them **Extend:** encourage children to invent more imaginative and appropriate dialogue for their characters
	Independent work Encourage the children to think carefully about the character they are going to play. What will they wear? What will they say? How will they move about?	
	Plenary Invite each group to re-enact the story while the other group watches. After the performances encourage helpful comments about developing the story further.	

DAY 2 ▪ Retelling the story

Key features	Stages	Additional opportunities
	Introduction Retell a familiar story to the children, such as *Not now, Bernard*. What did they enjoy about the experience? What is special about being told a story? Explain that you would like them to become storytellers, telling one another the story of *Amazing Grace*.	
	Speaking and listening Talk about the idea of retelling a story and discuss how the storyteller makes the story come to life by using different voices for the characters. Emphasise the importance of remembering things such as characters, settings and events. Display the character list created on Day 1 and add words associated with settings, such as home, school, theatre, and events such as ballet and pantomime. Do the children think this list will help them to retell the story?	
Social skills: listening to others and taking turns	**Independent work** Put the children into pairs to take turns to tell the story to one another, modifying or developing it after listening to their partner's version.	**Support:** provide picture prompts if necessary
Creative thinking: applying their imaginative ideas to portray story events	**Plenary** Bring the class together and let some children tell their stories to the others. Encourage the whole class to discuss their storytelling skills and ways in which they can develop them further.	**Extend:** encourage more descriptive words relating to settings and events

Guided reading

Ask the children to read simple words such as *up, had, act, just* by segmenting sounds into their constituent phonemes. Find and read more words in other books following this approach.

Display *Amazing Grace – extract 2* and reinforce children's awareness of HFW. Make up sentences using some of these words.

Assessment

Can the children re-enact a story taking on the character parts? Do they sequence the main events?

Refer back to the learning outcomes on page 11.

Further work

Show children who need a support a picture on a page and invite them to re-enact what is happening.

Extend children by asking them to invent voices and recreate dialogue for the characters.

DAY 1 ■ Telling stories based on personal experience

Key features	Stages	Additional opportunities
Social skills: sharing opinions	**Introduction** Ask the children to recall some of the characters they have met in the stories they have read in recent lessons. What did they like or dislike about them? List their names as headings on a large sheet and describe some of their individual characteristics underneath. Choose one of the characters and talk about some of the events this character was involved in.	
Communication: comparing experiences	**Speaking and listening** Read *Amazing Grace* and talk about the children's experiences of dressing up. Do they dress up at home? What do they put on? Who do they pretend to be? Explain that you are going to ask the children to think of a story about one of the characters they enjoy dressing up as. Display photocopiable page 30 'Character, setting, event'. Fill the first column with the children's names and then write each child's chosen character in the column alongside. Compile lists of possible settings and events in columns three and four.	
Communication: working collaboratively	**Independent work** Put the children into pairs to make up a short story together involving their two chosen characters. Explain that they can use the list compiled earlier for ideas for settings and events or invent their own. Allow them time to modify and develop the story.	**Support:** give additional support with building up words using phonics **Extend:** attempt to write the main events in their stories
	Plenary Bring the children together to tell their stories and discuss them with one another.	

DAY 2 ■ Modelling the writing

Key features	Stages	Additional opportunities
	Introduction Display the list compiled on Day 1 to remind children of their previous work on characters, settings and events. Ask them to recall the story ideas they developed. Explain that today they are going to listen to a poem about storybook characters and then write a story about one of them.	**Phonics:** box, socks
Creative thinking: applying imaginative ideas for drama and story writing	**Speaking and listening** Display the poem *Dressing up* from the CD-ROM and read this aloud to the children. Discuss the characters mentioned. Which one would they like to be? What would they wear? Can they think of a story idea involving their chosen character? Suggest that they think of their previous experiences of identifying characters, settings and events and any stories they remember about princes, princesses, wizards or witches to help them.	
	Independent work Divide the class into groups of four and provide each group with a selection of storybook character dressing-up clothes and associated props to help them dramatise their story ideas. Take a short video film of each group as they perform their dramatisations.	
	Plenary Bring the children together to watch the films. Choose one film and model how to write a sentence about the beginning, middle and end of the action. Explain that the children will be planning out their stories the next day.	**Extend and support:** write an extended and simplified version of the sentence

DAY 3 ◢ Talking for writing

Key features	Stages	Additional opportunities
	Introduction Remind the children of the discussions they had with their partners the day before. Can they recall their story idea? Explain that they are going to look at the films again to help them to think of a simple story plan.	
Social skills: listening to and respecting ideas **Motivation:** having a clear goal for independent writing	**Speaking and listening** Choose one film and encourage the children involved to tell the others what is happening. Discuss what happens at the beginning, middle and end of the story and demonstrate how to write three simple sentences to identify this sequence. Read the sentences aloud and then ask the children to do so. Ask the children to go into the same groups again to work together to draw pictures and write sentences about their stories. Encourage them to consider the sequence of events and the characters involved.	**Extend:** encourage word recognition by including HFW
	Independent work While the other groups are writing, ask groups to take turns to use a digital camera to photograph one another dressed up as characters from their story striking a suitable pose.	
Evaluation: giving feedback to others and judging their own writing	**Plenary** Ask the groups to take turns to hold up their pictures in sequence and read their sentences to the others. Discuss the story ideas these groups have created.	

DAY 4 ◢ Storyboarding

Key features	Stages	Additional opportunities
Social skills: taking turns and sharing	**Introduction** Explain that in this lesson children will be using a storyboard to help plan out the sequence of events for their story. Show them the photographs they took during the last lesson and explain that they might also be useful for their plans.	
Creative thinking: applying imaginative ideas to create ideas for story writing **Communication:** collaborative exchange of ideas	**Speaking and listening** Tell the children that they are going to use a storyboard to plan the story they discussed in the last lesson. Display photocopiable page 29 'The gardener's diary' and remind them of stories they planned in Sequence 1 using this page. Explain that you are going to provide them with a similar page to plan out the beginning, middle and end of their own story. Put the children into the same groups and supply them with the photographs they took and a page showing three boxes with space around them. Invite the children to look at the photographs to decide on a sentence to write in each box depicting events that happen at first, in the middle and at the end of their stories. Invite them to draw pictures in the boxes and decorate around them.	**Support:** write a few relevant words rather than a sentence **Support:** apply phonic knowledge and skills when reading sentences
Evaluation: discussing criteria for written work	**Independent work** Ask the groups to read their storyboards to each other, with one child saying what the story is about and the others reading a sentence each. After listening, decide on any modifications to produce a final version.	**Extend:** create more detailed storyboards for favourite stories
	Plenary Bring the children back together and discuss how they might use their plans and photographs to write their storybook.	

DAY 5 ◼ Writing the story

Key features	Stages	Additional opportunities
Social skills: listening to and respecting other people's story ideas	## Introduction Talk about the ways in which the children have prepared for writing a story, such as sharing favourite memories, dressing up as characters, writing sentences, taking photographs and planning storyboards. Say that you feel that they are now ready to write a storybook themselves.	
Creative thinking: applying imaginative ideas to enhance story writing	## Speaking and listening Put the children into the same groups and give out their storyboards, photographs, and three sheets of paper. Ask them to use the resources to make a book, remembering what they have learned in previous lessons. This time encourage children to make individual books rather than a class book, designing and making their own book covers.	**Extend:** add additional pages to develop the story
Evaluation: giving feedback and beginning to judge the effectiveness of their writing	## Independent work Have one group read their story to another so that they can modify and develop their ideas and judge the effectiveness of their writing. ## Plenary Hold up and read some of the finished books and talk about similarities and differences in content. Display them where children can read them independently.	

Guided reading
Encourage children to apply phonic knowledge and skills when reading sentences aloud.

Assessment
Use the 'Story structure' assessment activity from the CD-ROM. Can the children to write three simple sentences and make these into a storybook?
Refer back to the learning outcomes on page 11.

Further work
Give extra help with simple sentence construction to children who need it. Extend children by asking them to design covers and add additional pages to their books.

Oliver's vegetables

100 LITERACY FRAMEWORK LESSONS YEAR 1

PHOTOCOPIABLE

SCHOLASTIC
www.scholastic.co.uk

Storybook characters

Illustrations © Andy Keylock / Beehive Illustration.

The growing sequence of a pea

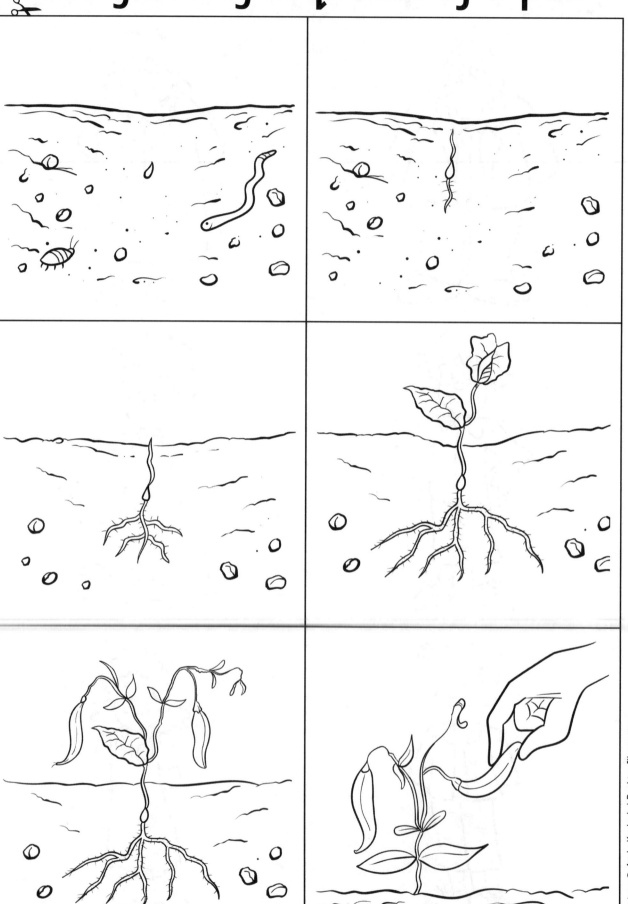

PHOTOCOPIABLE ■SCHOLASTIC
www.scholastic.co.uk

Illustrations © Andy Keylock / Beehive Illustration.

The gardener's diary

At the beginning I...

Then, a few weeks later I...

In the end I...

Character, setting, event

■ Use this chart to note your story ideas.

Name	Character	Setting	Event

NARRATIVE
UNIT 2 Stories from a range of cultures

Speak and listen for range of purposes on paper and on screen

Strand 1 Speaking
■ Interpret a text by reading aloud with some variety in pace and emphasis.
Strand 2 Listening and responding
■ Listen with sustained concentration, building new stores of words in different contexts.
Strand 3 Group discussion and interaction
■ Take turns to speak, listen to others' suggestions and talk about what they are going to do.
■ Explain their views to others in a small group, decide how to report the group's views to the class.

Read for a range of purposes on paper and on screen

Strand 5 Word recognition: decoding (reading) and encoding (spelling)
■ Apply phonic knowledge and skills as the prime approach to reading and spelling unfamiliar words that are not completely decodable.
Strand 6 Word structure and spelling
■ Spell new words using phonics as the prime approach.
Strand 7 Understanding and interpreting texts
■ Identify the main events and characters in stories, and find specific information in simple texts.
■ Use syntax and context when reading for meaning.
■ Explain the effect of patterns of language and repeated words and phrases.
Strand 8 Engaging and responding to texts
■ Select books for personal reading and give reasons for choices.

Write for a range of purposes on paper and on screen

Strand 9 Creating and shaping texts
■ Independently choose what to write about, plan and follow it through.
■ Use key features of narrative in their own writing.
■ Find and use new and interesting words and phrases, including story language.
Strand 10 Text structure and organisation
■ Write chronological and non-chronological texts using simple structures.
Strand 11 Sentence structure and punctuation
■ Compose and write simple sentences independently to communicate meaning.
■ Use capital letters and full stops when punctuating simple sentences.
Strand 12 Presentation
■ Write most letters, correctly formed and orientated, using a comfortable and efficient pencil grip.

Progression in narrative

In this year, children are moving towards:
■ Listening to and reading a range of stories on page and screen which provoke different responses; listening with sustained concentration and then talking about how the author created interest or excitement in the story; recognising that settings can be familiar or unfamiliar and based on real-life or fantasy.
■ Creating stories orally, on page and screen, that will impact on listeners and readers in a range of ways; retelling familiar stories and recounting events;

▶

using story language to organise events.
■ Writing complete stories with a simple structure: beginning – middle – end, deciding where it is set and using ideas from reading for some events.

Key aspects of learning covered in this Unit

Empathy
Children will learn about other worlds and consider the thoughts, feelings and actions of characters.

Creative thinking
Children will use their imaginations as they create new ways of using and extending familiar patterns for new stories.

Social skills
Children will learn about taking turns, listening to others and trying to reach agreement as they work together in a group.

Communication
Children will develop their ability to discuss as they work collaboratively in paired, group and whole-class contexts. They will communicate outcomes orally, in writing and through ICT if appropriate.

Prior learning

Before starting this Unit check that the children can:
■ Experiment with sounds, words and texts when making up their own stories and rhymes.
■ Take turns in group discussions.
■ Identify the characters, settings and main events in a story.
■ Write a complete sentence using a capital letter and a full stop.
If they need further support refer to a prior Unit or to the Foundation Stage.

Resources

Sequence 1, Phase 1: A version of 'Chicken Licken'; *The gingerbread man* by Jean Evans ✺; *So much* by Trish Cooke (Walker), *So much – extract 1* ✺; Dolls; A version of 'The Enormous Turnip'; Roll of wallpaper
Sequence 1, Phase 2: *Handa's Hen* by Eileen Browne (Walker); A version of 'The three little pigs'
Sequence 1, Phase 3: *So much* by Trish Cooke (Walker); *So much – extract 2* ✺; *Elephant Dance* by Theresa Heine (Barefoot)
Sequence 1, Phase 4: Photocopiable page 49 'My storyboard'
Sequence 2, Phase 1: *The Elephant and the Bad Baby* by Elfrida Dupont (Puffin); *The Other Ark* by Lynley Dodd (Puffin); Photocopiable page 50 'Rhyming words 1'; Photocopiable page 51 'Rhyming words 2'; *The Other Ark* extract ✺
Sequence 2, Phase 2: Photocopiable page 52 'Fantasy creatures'; *The Other Ark* extract ✺
Sequence 2, Phase 3: *Eat Up, Gemma* by Sarah Hayes (Walker); A traditional version of 'Noah's Ark'; *The Other Ark* extract ✺; Picture of an ark ✺
Sequence 2, Phase 4: *The Other Ark* extract ✺; Photocopiable page 49 'My storyboard'; A range of familiar storybooks; Assessment activity 'The little gingerbread man' ✺

Cross-curricular opportunities

Geography (other countries and cultures)
PSHE (Bible stories – Noah's Ark, family events)

UNIT 2 ■ Teaching sequence 1

Phase	Children's objectives	Summary of activities	Learning outcomes
1	I can explore stories with patterned language. I can explore stories with patterned language from other cultures. I can join in with stories with patterned language.	Retell 'The Gingerbread Man' in pairs. Join in with repeated phrases. Join in with phrases from *So much*. Exploring repetition in 'The Enormous Turnip'.	Children can join in and recite parts of stories with predictable and patterned language, including those from other cultures, and discuss their effect.
2	I can invent and write new sentences based on story patterns. I can adapt familiar stories using familiar and patterned language.	Write new sentences using language patterns from *Handa's Hen*. Write class adaptation of 'The Three Little Pigs'.	Children can explore, adapt, invent and write sentences or lines based on patterns in familiar stories.
3	I can discuss familiar and unfamiliar aspects of a book. I can compare familiar and unfamiliar aspects of a range of books.	Explore aspects of *So much* and compare with own lives. Explore *Elephant Dance* as a class and another book of their choice in pairs.	Children can discuss familiar and unfamiliar aspects of a book and identify patterns in the text.
4	I can use written notes to plan a story. I can use patterned and repetitive language when writing a story. I can write down a new story.	Choose a story to support ideas for a new story. Write catchphrases and repeated sentences based on a chosen story. Write their story using their ideas from Days 1 and 2.	Children can write simple sentences using patterned language, words and phrases taken from familiar stories.

UNIT 2 ■ Teaching sequence 2

Phase	Children's objectives	Summary of activities	Learning outcomes
1	I can share a story with patterned language. I can identify rhyme in a story with patterned language. I can recognise rhymes and repetition in a story.	Discover pattern and repetition in *The Elephant and the Bad Baby*. Find rhyming words in a book and on a worksheet. Look for repetition in *The Other Ark*.	Children recognise language patterns and repeated words and phrases in a text, including those from other cultures, and discuss their effect on a reader.
2	I can invent new character names. I can invent a new story based on familiar patterned language.	Write new creature names by mixing and matching animal names. Write sentences for a new story based on *The Other Ark*.	Children can write their own sentences based on patterned language from a familiar text.
3	I can explore a patterned text from another culture. I can compare traditional and new versions of a story.	Explore the story *Eat up, Gemma* and compare aspects with their own lives. Compare traditional and new versions of the story of 'Noah's Ark'.	Children can work as part of a group, taking turns and sharing ideas, listening to others and reporting their findings.
4	I can use a familiar story as a model for planning a new story. I can use repeated language when writing a story. I can write the middle of the story and incorporate it into the whole story.	Note-making based on *The Other Ark* for the middle of a new story. Write catchphrases or repeated lines for the middle of a story. Write the whole story together.	Children can write simple sentences using patterned language, words and phrases taken from familiar stories.

Provide copies of the objectives for the children.

DAY 1 ■ Exploring stories with predictable and patterned language

Key features	Stages	Additional opportunities
	Introduction Read the traditional story of 'Chicken Licken' to the children and ask them to identify the repeated sentence, *The sky is falling and we are going to tell the king.* Invite them to join in with familiar parts of the story. Explain that this story is easy to remember because of the repetition and rhyming names.	**Phonics:** Chicken Licken, Ducky Lucky **HFW:** down, going, as, can't, little, old, water, very, good
Empathy: considering the thoughts and feelings of the main character	**Speaking and listening** Display *The gingerbread man* from the CD-ROM and invite the children to identify the repeated sentence. Read through the story, highlighting the sentence as it appears in the text. Ask questions about what happens at the beginning and end of the story.	**Support:** read the story to small groups and ask them to say the repeated line
Communication: working collaboratively	**Independent work** Put the children into pairs and ask them to recall the story, with one partner saying the words of the gingerbread man and the other telling the sequence of events in the story, trying to remember the characters in the correct order.	**Extend:** tell the story of 'Chicken Licken'
	Plenary Bring the children together and ask some pairs to tell the story. How accurate are their versions? Did they remember the predictable language? Tell the story to the children again, asking them to join in as much as possible.	

DAY 2 ■ Exploring stories with patterned language from other cultures

Key features	Stages	Additional opportunities
	Introduction Read the story *So much* to the children and ask them to listen for repetitive phrases and sentences in the story, such as *They weren't doing anything, nothing really..., Then, DING DONG!, It was..., So much!* Discuss how the story follows this pattern with the number of people involved growing until Daddy appears for his birthday party. Display *So much – extract 1* from the CD-ROM showing Mum and the baby looking out of the window and ask the children to read the words together.	**Phonics:** ding dong **Extend:** explore the use of capital letters to show that the repeated phrases DING DONG, So much should be read with more emphasis
Empathy: learning about other worlds		
Communication: working collaboratively	**Speaking and listening** Ask the children to help you make a list of main characters, events and key phrases. Explore the characters' names, their clothes and appearance and compare them with those of the children. Repeat the key phrases.	
Creative thinking: using their imaginations to extend familiar patterns for their own stories	**Independent work** Put the children into pairs to retell the story to one another, using the list they have made and including the repeated phrases. Supply each group with a doll to represent the baby. Explain that the story does not need to have exactly the same words; repeating the sequence of characters in order and saying key phrases will be sufficient.	
	Plenary Bring the class back together to tell their stories before reading the story to the whole group, asking them to join in as much as possible.	

DAY 3 ■ Joining in with stories with predictable and patterned language

Key features	Stages	Additional opportunities
	Introduction Choose a familiar story with a predictable pattern, such as 'The Enormous Turnip', and tell or read the story to the children. What do they notice about the predictable pattern of the words? How effective is this? Explain that the sequence of events is similar to those in *So much*, with the number of characters growing until the final event of the story, when the turnip is uprooted.	**Phonics:** pulled, turnip **HFW:** once, little, could not, boy, girl, man, old, pull
	Speaking and listening Read the story again, this time writing the names of the characters as they appear in the story. Once all of the characters have been listed, tell the story using this list and the repeated phrase, *And the little old man pulled...* adding the next character each time.	
Creative thinking: using imaginations to create new ways of using familiar patterns for stories	**Independent work** Roll out a length of wallpaper and write the names of the characters in the story in the correct sequence along it at spaced intervals. Divide the children into equal groups, each responsible for drawing either the enormous turnip or one of the characters. Once the sequence is complete, invite the groups to sit next to their drawings to retell the story.	**Extend:** write an appropriate sentence under each character
	Plenary Recall the stories explored over the last three days. What do they have in common? Can the children remember any of the repeated phrases in them? Would the stories be as effective if the patterned language was removed?	**Support:** focus on one story to discuss rather than several

Guided reading

Encourage children to recognise an increasing number of HFW in the story texts used.
Use segmenting and blending skills and phoneme/grapheme knowledge to read and spell the phonically decodable names of the characters in 'Chicken Licken'.

Assessment

Do the children identify language patterns and talk about their effect on the reader? Can they join in with repeated phrases and sentences in a story as they listen to it?
Refer back to the learning outcomes on page 33.

Further work

Ask children to make up their own stories for others to join in with, using similar patterns of language.

DAY 1 ▪ Inventing and writing new sentences based on story patterns

Key features	Stages	Additional opportunities
Empathy: learning about other worlds	### Introduction Read a story such as *Handa's Hen* and ask the children if they can identify a pattern in the story. Ask the children to identify the repetitive language. Read the story again and ask the children to join in with this phrase. Identify how the number of creatures Handa finds on her search for Mondi increases by one each time.	**Phonics:** *Handa, help, hen* **HFW:** numbers to ten, house, where, little
Communication: working collaboratively	### Independent work Demonstrate how to write a list of the main characters and events in the story, asking the children to help with spelling. Refer to the book and list to explore the names of the characters, their clothes and appearance and compare them with the children in the class. Ask the children to create their own story using repetitive language, based on the story you read in the introduction.	**Support:** limit the number of items found to two **Extend:** invite more confident children to write more detailed sentences
Social skills: taking turns, listening and reaching agreement	### Plenary Bring the class back together to read out their stories. Discuss modifying them in order to make patterned language and repeated phrases more effective.	

DAY 2 ▪ Adapting familiar stories using predictable and patterned language

Key features	Stages	Additional opportunities
	### Introduction Ask the children to recall the stories they made up about Handa and Mondi. Talk about how the predictable text and familiar patterns helped them.	**Phonics:** *pig, let, in, chin, chinny, huff, puff* **HFW:** three, little, by
	### Speaking and listening Tell or read a traditional version of 'The Three Little Pigs' and ask the children to help you to write the main events in sequence, such as leaving home and building houses, asking for help with spelling as you do so. Identify repeated phrases such as: *Little pig, little pig let me come in, No, no by the hair on my chinny chin chin, I'll huff and I'll puff...* Add these to the events list and keep a copy. Explain that the children are going to write their own version of the story, using this list to help them.	
Creative thinking: using their imaginations to create new stories based on familiar patterns	### Independent work Put the children into groups and allocate one event from the list to each group. Ask the children in the group to draw a picture of the event and write short sentences about it, using their own ideas based on phrases from the list compiled as a class. Encourage them to say sentences before writing. Explain that they will be putting their sentences together to create a class story.	**Support:** encourage use of capital letters and full stops, support correct letter formation and word spacing
Communication: discussing their work collaboratively	### Plenary Bring the class together and invite each group to read out their sentences in the correct sequence. Comment on the patterns in the language used. Which words and phrases have they repeated?	

Guided reading

Support punctuation and sentence structure. Encourage correct letter formation and spaces between words. Draw attention to HFW for numbers one to ten.

Assessment

Can children adapt and invent sentences or lines based on patterns in familiar stories?
Can they write down these sentences?
Refer back to the learning outcomes on page 33.

Further work

Ask the children to write a short story using a predictable language or a familiar pattern.

DAY 1 ■ Discussing familiar and unfamiliar aspects of a book

Key features	Stages	Additional opportunities
Empathy: learning about other worlds	**Introduction** Read *So much* and talk about what is familiar and unfamiliar about the story, for example, the language used. Display *So much – extract 2* showing the image of Uncle Didi and the baby. Discuss their appearance and read the text. Draw attention to the rich rhythm of Afro-Caribbean speech in other parts of the book, for example, *He give the baby pinch and the baby give him slap. Would the text sound the same if it read* he pinched the baby and the baby slapped him back? Clap the rhythm of each sentence. Which sounds best?	**Phonics:** Oooooooh!, Mmmmmmm, Aieeeeee!, Yoooooo hoooooo, Zzzzzzz, huh huh
Social skills: working collaboratively	**Independent work** Write down key headings about the book, such as: *Family members, The party, The baby, Clothes, Actions*. Encourage the children to explore one aspect of the book with a partner. Supply each pair with a sheet of paper folded down the middle with one of the headings at the top of each half. Invite them to write words about the book on one side and their own experiences on the other and compare the two lists.	**Support:** draw one picture and write a word in each column, for example, to compare their Mum with the baby's Mum
Communication: taking turns and listening to others	**Plenary** Bring the children together to share their lists and discuss the book again. Do they notice any more detail after their discussions?	**Extend:** suggest their own headings

DAY 2 ■ Comparing familiar and unfamiliar aspects of a range of books

Key features	Stages	Additional opportunities
	Introduction Ask the children to recall their exploration of *So much* the day before. Display the extract from the CD-ROM as a prompt and explain that they are going to explore another book in a similar way.	**Phonics:** hot, hotter, red, gold, golden, silver, yellow, green
Empathy: learning about other worlds	**Speaking and listening** Read a story which features another culture, such as *Elephant Dance*. Identify the main character and briefly discuss the country or culture of the story. *Elephant Dance* has maps of India in the centre of the book. Compare the story with *So Much*. Identify any unfamiliar words with the children. In *Elephant Dance* Ravi's Grandfather uses lots of exciting words to describe the sun, wind, rain and snow.	**Support:** use simplified language to help children understand this rich language
	Independent work Put the children into pairs and provide a range of storybooks, including some from other cultures, for them to choose from. Ask them to discuss a book , saying what is familiar and unfamiliar about the illustrations and any of the text they can read. Encourage them to write down words for later discussion.	**Extend:** decode more challenging texts using acquired phonic knowledge and skills
Communication: discussing and giving personal opinions	**Plenary** Bring the class together and invite pairs of children to tell the others about their book. What did they like about it? What was familiar? What was unfamiliar?	

Guided reading
Use repetition of graphemes in *So much* such as *ooooooo, zzzzzz* and *mmmmmm* to emphasise the phonemes created. Encourage children to use their acquired phonic knowledge and skills and automatic recognition of HFW to read and compare a wide range of books.

Assessment
Can the children discuss familiar and unfamiliar aspects of a book and identify patterns in the text? Refer back to the learning outcomes on page 33.

Further work
Supply more challenging texts for children to read for discussion.

DAY 1 ▪ Using written notes to plan a story

Key features	Stages	Additional opportunities
	Introduction Display copies of the stories the children have focused on recently and ask them to choose one of them to give them ideas for a new story.	
Social skills: taking turns, listening and sharing ideas	**Speaking and listening** Ask the children to recall what happened at the beginning of their chosen story. Make a note of significant words used by the children. Do the same with words relating to the middle and end of the story. Explain that you are going to tell the children a new story using these notes to help. When you have told the story, ask them to think of ways to help you to make it more interesting, for example, by extending dialogue or using more descriptive words.	**Extend:** write descriptive words about a character
Creative thinking: using their imaginations to create new stories	**Independent work** Divide the children into small groups and ask each group to choose a displayed book to give them story ideas. Give the children photocopiable page 49 'My storyboard' to write notes about the beginning, middle and end of their story.	**Support:** use drama to help them to tell their stories
	Plenary Bring the class together to share their notes and ideas and tell their stories. How are they different from the original story? How are they similar? Discuss together how the stories might be extended.	

DAY 2 ▪ Using patterned and repetitive language when writing a story

Key features	Stages	Additional opportunities
	Introduction Remind the children of the notes they wrote in the previous lesson and explain that they are going to use these along with new language to write their stories.	
	Speaking and listening Display the notes you made with the class about a chosen story. Say that these notes will help them to remember the beginning, middle and end of the story. Can they remember any patterned language or repetitions from the story? Talk about why the children think this sort of language is effective in stories.	
Creative thinking: using imaginations to adapt familiar language patterns	**Independent work** Ask the children to go back into the groups they were in for the last lesson so that they can continue to write their stories. Remind them that the story they are writing will be similar to their chosen story in some ways, but as it will be written by them it should have differences too. Suggest that they think of different ways of using patterned language, perhaps by giving a character a catchphrase or by changing a repeated line. Ask the children to think about some ideas for catchphrases or repeated lines and write their ideas down to share with the class.	**Support:** suggest appropriate one word changes **Extend:** adapt interesting words and phrases that appeal to them to use in their own stories
Communication: discussing and modifying their work collaboratively	**Plenary** Bring the class back together and ask the groups to take turns to introduce examples of their catchphrase, patterned language or repeated lines. Discuss the ideas together and make suggestions for developments.	

DAY 3 ■ Writing down a new story

Key features	Stages	Additional opportunities

Introduction
Discuss the plans the children have made for writing a story over the last two lessons, noting appropriate words and making up new repetitive language based on a familiar story. Tell them that they are going to write down their stories to read to the rest of the class.

Speaking and listening
Organise the children go into the same groups again and provide them with their written ideas from Days 1 and 2. Supply them with the paper to form the pages of their storybook, talk them through the stages of writing and illustrating a beginning, middle and end page and explain that they can write additional pages if they wish to. Ask them to describe what their story is going to be about.

Creative thinking: using imaginations to extend familiar patterns in their stories

Independent work
As the children are working, draw their attention to their use of patterned language and encourage them to make use of their knowledge of phonics and awareness of high frequency words. Talk about ways of combining words with images on the page.

Support: talk to children about how they will write down words, using phonics as the prime approach

Plenary
Bring the class together to read their stories to one another. Discuss similarities between the stories and the originals. Have the children used or adapted patterned language and words and phrases based on these originals? Could the stories could be modified? Display the stories on a large board.

Communication: communicating orally and in writing

Extend: create individual books with covers and a title

Guided reading
Focus on developing sentence structure and punctuation by asking children to consider whether their sentences communicate meaning and encouraging correct use of capital letters and full stops.

Assessment
Can children write simple sentences using patterned language, words and phrases taken from familiar stories? Refer back to the learning outcomes on page 33.

Further work
Make children's pages into individual books and read or recite them together.

DAY 1 ■ Sharing a story with predictable and patterned language

Key features	Stages	Additional opportunities
	### Introduction Remind the children of previous stories they have enjoyed with predictable and patterned language such as 'The Gingerbread Man' and 'The Enormous Turnip'. Why is it easy to remember these stories? Can the children recall any of the repeated lines? Read a story with a repeated line such as *The Elephant and the Bad Baby*. Are there any repeated words that make this book special? Discuss how in *The Elephant and the Bad Baby* an elephant makes a trumpeting sound and so the word *rumpeta* is especially effective.	**Phonics:** yes, put, him, went, met, bad, running **HFW:** would, down **Extend:** take turns to read the repeated lines aloud
	### Speaking and listening Explore other aspects of repetition in the story. For example: What sentence follows every time the elephant asks the baby a question? Read the story and ask the children to join in whenever they can. Can the children think of other stories that are similar to the chosen story?	**Support:** re-read the story, pausing to allow time for children to join in with repeated lines
Creative thinking: talking imaginatively about their ideas	### Independent work Ask the children to sit with a partner to discuss the story. What did they like about it? Which words, phrases or patterns were most effective?	
Communication: discussing their ideas as a group	### Plenary Bring the children together again and have one partner tell the others about the other partner's thoughts. Did any children like the same aspects?	

DAY 2 ■ Identifying rhyme in a story

Key features	Stages	Additional opportunities
Social skills: speaking about their likes and dislikes and listening to others sharing theirs	### Introduction Read *The Other Ark* and ask the children what they like or dislike about the story. Read the first page again, stressing the rhyming words. Ask the children to tap the rhythm softly while you read. Did they notice the regular beat?	**Phonics:** ark, dark, mark, flumps, humps, cats, spats, spot, dot **HFW:** must, these, door, more, take, were, with, old
	### Speaking and listening Explain that this story sounds so satisfying when it is read aloud because of the regular rhymes at the end of the sentences. Ask the children to choose one of the pages to hear again and ask them to identify the rhyming words. Write these on a screen or large sheet of paper. Encourage children to recognise that phonemes can have alternative representations, for example, in the words *do*, *blew*, *Balu* and draw attention to any high frequency words.	**Extend:** read and spell phonically decodable two-syllable and three-syllable words such as *bucketed*, *teeming*
Communication: working collaboratively to complete a task	### Independent work Put the children into pairs and give each pair a copy of photocopiable page 50 'Rhyming words 1' (support) or page 51 'Rhyming words 2' (extension). Ask the children to find the pairs of rhyming words.	
	### Plenary Bring the class back together, look at their completed sheets and read the story of *The Other Ark* together, writing down rhyming words as they are identified by the children. Invite them to think of additional words that finish with the same sounds.	

DAY 3 ■ Recognising effectiveness of patterns and repetition in a story

Key features	Stages	Additional opportunities
Social skills: listening to each other's thoughts and memories	### Introduction Display *The Other Ark* extract from the CD-ROM and ask the children to identify the story this sequence is from. What can they remember about the story? Who are the main characters? ### Speaking and listening Read the displayed text aloud and talk about the language used. Ask the children to identify the rhyming words *Balu*, *blew* and *do*. What sound does each word finish with? Reinforce work from Day 2 on alternative representation of phonemes. Read the story aloud and ask the children to anticipate and join in with each rhyming word by listening carefully as you read, for example, *look at the mud, ...here comes the fl... .* Highlight the last four lines of the text on screen and explain the meaning of *A1 efficient*. Look through the book to find out how many times these lines are repeated. Ask the children to say the words aloud as you point to them.	**Phonics:** t*a*sk, S*a*m J*a*m, p*u*shed, p*u*lled, p*u*ffed, tr*i*cky, Bal*u*, bl*ew*, d*o*, m*u*d, fl*oo*d **HFW:** what, there, too
Creative thinking: using imaginations to draw their favourite creatures from a story and write their names	### Independent work Put the children into pairs and ask individuals to draw a picture of their favourite creature from the story and write its name underneath. Ask them to discuss their drawings with their partners and add extra detail they might have forgotten. ### Plenary Look at the children's drawings together and talk about where the creatures appear in the story. Read the story, asking children to join in when they can.	**Support:** remember and write the name of their chosen creature **Extend:** write a rhyme about their favourite creature

Guided reading
Draw attention to rhyming words in the chosen texts. Encourage children to realise that phonemes can have alternative representations.
Find examples of repetition of words and phrases and read them together.

Assessment
Can the children recognise language patterns, rhymes and repeated words and phrases in a text and discuss their effect on the reader?
Refer back to the learning outcomes on page 33.

Further work
Invite small groups of children to have similar discussions about other popular stories.

DAY 1 ◼ Making up new story characters

Key features	Stages	Additional opportunities
	Introduction Read *The Other Ark* and ask the children to recall some of the creatures that Sam Jam Balu takes into Noah's alternative ark. Have they ever heard of any of these creatures? Look carefully at the illustrations. Do they look familiar or unfamiliar? Some of them have familiar names, such as hippo and camel, but look very different. Explain that the author has imagined them all for her story.	**Phonics:** *hip-hopping* hippos, fl*u*mps, comical h*u*mps, carnival c*a*ts, butternut
	Speaking and listening Look through the book together and make a list of the creatures. Talk about how some creatures are combinations of others, such as kangaroosters, elephant snails and alligatigers.	
Creative thinking: use their imaginations to create new characters based on a familiar story	**Independent work** Put the children into pairs and explain that they are going to play a mix and match game to help them with ideas for a new creature to go into the ark. Provide each pair with photocopiable page 52 'Fantasy creatures' and ask them to cut out the creatures and match them together in unusual ways. Suggest that they choose one of the creatures, or make up an entirely different one and think of a name for it.	**Support:** help children to make up one name from two creatures, such as *horse-snail* **Extend:** make up two-syllable and three-syllable names using knowledge of phonics
	Plenary Bring the class back together to show their creatures and talk about them. Explain that they will put them into their own story of Noah's ark on Day 2.	

DAY 2 ◼ Inventing a new story based on familiar patterned language

Key features	Stages	Additional opportunities
	Introduction Give out the children's drawings of the characters they invented on Day 1 and explain that they are going to use them in the new story they are writing.	**Phonics:** pulled, gangplank, noon, dot, stuck, spot
	Speaking and listening Read *The Other Ark* again and talk about the sequence of events. What happened when Noah's first ark was full? Read the last page together and discuss how the story finishes. Suggest that the new story follows this pattern.	
Creative thinking: using their imaginations to create new sentences	**Independent work** Arrange the children back into pairs with their drawings and ask them to think of action words to describe how their creature will get into the ark, for example, will they hop, skip, jump, slither, slide, fly or teeter? Ask them to write a sentence to describe this movement always starting with the words; *Into the ark* for example, *Into the ark the eleworm slithered, slimy and grimy and green.*	**Support:** use phonically regular words such as *run, jump, hop, skip* **Extend:** use imaginative words such as *teetered* and *wibbled*
Communication: comparing their story with the original	**Plenary** Display *The Other Ark* extract from the CD-ROM showing the old ark with lots of windows and a gangplank. Bring the class together and begin to tell the story by reading the displayed text. Invite each pair to come out, read their sentence, move their creature picture up the gangplank and stick it onto one of the windows. Are the children satisfied with their new story? How does it differ from the original?	

Guided reading and writing

Help children to read and spell phonically decodable two-syllable and three-syllable words. Encourage them to find and use new and interesting words and phrases for their story writing.

Assessment

Can children write their own sentences based on patterns in familiar stories?

Refer back to the learning outcomes on page 33.

Further work

Ask children to choose another story with predictable and patterned language and use this as a basis for writing a similar story of their own.

DAY 1 ■ Exploring a patterned text

Key features	Stages	Additional opportunities
Empathy: learning about other worlds	**Introduction** Read a story from another culture such as *Eat up, Gemma* and talk about the language used. Ask: *Who is the main character? What happens in the story?* **Speaking and listening** Read the story again and look at the illustrations on each page. Identify what is familiar and unfamiliar about the characters, settings and events. For example does Gemma have a big or small family? Are there similarities and differences between the way Gemma's family look and dress and the children look and dress? Identify the repeated phrase throughout the book.	**Phonics:** did*n't*. could*n't*, would*n't*, was*n't* **Support:** talk children through the events, using the phrase *Eat up, Gemma*
Social skills: working together to reach agreement	**Independent work** Provide groups of children with books about different cultures that use patterned language. Ask each group to choose two to look at. Encourage them to discuss what is familiar or unfamiliar and to look for patterns.	**Extend:** write down the result of their discussion in note form
Social skills: taking turns	**Plenary** Bring the children together to report their findings to one another.	

DAY 2 ■ Comparing versions of a story

Key features	Stages	Additional opportunities
	Introduction Explain that you are going to read two versions of 'Noah's Ark' and you would like the children to notice things that are the same and different about them.	
Communication: reaching a collaborative decision on their favourite book	**Speaking and listening** Read a traditional version of Noah's Ark and discuss the main characters, settings and events. Read *The Other Ark* and do the same. How do the characters and animals vary in the two stories? Display the picture of a traditional ark from the CD-ROM. How does *The Other Ark* compare with this traditional ark? Talk about similar events in the story, such as the creatures entering the ark in twos, and very different events, such as the story endings.	**Support:** help children to write words using their phonic knowledge and awareness of HFW
	Independent work Put the children into small groups and ask them to choose a book about Noah's Ark. Ask them to talk about what is familiar and unfamiliar about the words and pictures. Encourage them to write down words for later discussion. **Plenary** Bring the class together. Invite groups to tell the others about what they have discovered. Decide upon a favourite version together and read this to the class.	**Extend:** encourage children to refer to words they have written earlier during discussion

Guided reading
Encourage children to read words using their phonic knowledge and awareness of HFW. Help children to read the words *wouldn't*, *couldn't* and *wasn't* in the story *Eat up, Gemma* using their knowledge of HFW.

Assessment
Can children work as a group to compare aspects of a book together, such as language used and characterisation, and then feedback their findings to the class?
Refer back to the learning outcomes on page 33.

Further work
Provide a more contrasting range of books for children to read and discuss.

DAY 1 ◾ Using a familiar story as a model for planning a new story

Key features	Stages	Additional opportunities
	Introduction Display *The Other Ark* extract from the CD-ROM and ask the children to recall what happens in the story. Explain that you are making up a new but similar story to tell them, for example, about a large family preparing for a sailing holiday, and have made notes about it. Display your story outline as notes showing the beginning, middle and end of the story.	
Creative thinking: expressing their imaginative ideas orally and through drama	**Speaking and listening** Begin to tell the story using the notes, asking the children how they might enhance the middle of your story. Invite them to take on the roles of any new characters they would like to introduce and to re-enact events they wish to include. Add the children's ideas to your notes in the appropriate box. Tell the final story and make comparisons between your story and the original.	
Communication: discussing their ideas collaboratively	**Independent work** Put the children into pairs and supply each pair with photocopiable page 49 'My storyboard' with the top and bottom boxes filled in with your story idea. Ask them to fill in the middle box with the ideas they developed in their discussions.	**Support:** draw a picture in each box and write single words about it
Communication: discussing ways of developing their ideas as a class	**Plenary** Bring the class together to share their ideas and tell modified stories. What are the similarities and differences in the stories? Could they be developed further?	**Extend:** use story language

DAY 2 ◾ Planning catchphrases and repeated lines for the story

Key features	Stages	Additional opportunities
	Introduction Ask the children to think of the stories they were planning the day before and the notes that they made. Did they include any ideas for catchphrases or repeated lines? Discuss the effect of such language.	
Communication: Discussing their sentences and suggesting modifications	**Speaking and listening** Ask the children to go into the same pairs again. Give out their story notes from the last lesson and suggest that they take turns to use their notes to make up a sentence and say it aloud to the rest of the class. Discuss the sentence. Could it be made more interesting, perhaps by using repetition?	
Creative thinking: using imaginations to create new ways of using familiar patterns	**Independent work** Invite the children to think of a catchphrase to put into the middle of the story. Suggest that they write down one or two ideas, in note form or simple sentences. While they are working, invite pairs to take turns to complete the interactive activity, 'The animals went in two by two' from the CD-ROM.	**Support:** help children put ideas into sentences **Extend:** use appropriate sentence structure and punctuation
	Plenary Bring the children together and ask them to read out their catchphrases or repeated lines to one another. Encourage them to comment and suggest modifications. Which ones do they think are easiest to remember?	

DAY 3 ■ Writing the middle of the story and completing the whole story

Key features	Stages	Additional opportunities
	Introduction Look at some familiar storybooks, read individual sentences aloud and discuss the meaning they convey. Remind the children that a sentence always starts with a capital letter and ends with a full stop, and point out how words are spaced to help the reader.	
Social skills: taking turns to listen to each other	**Speaking and listening** Ask the children to recall the notes they made on Day 1 and the catchphrases and repeated lines they created on Day 2. Explain that they are going to use this work to help them to write down the middle of the new story in sentences similar to the ones they have just explored.	
Creative thinking: using imaginations to create part of a story	**Independent work** Put the children into the same pairs and provide them with their notes and patterned language ideas from Days 1 and 2, and some sheets of paper. Encourage them to rehearse each sentence before writing it down and to keep re-reading the sentences after they have written them. Encourage them to talk to one another about alternative ways of expressing the same meaning and ask them to think about where and when they will use their catchphrase or repeated language.	**Support:** draw a picture of the middle of the story and, with adult help, choose words to write about it **Extend:** illustrate the book cover and write a title
	Plenary Bring the class together to read their writing to one another. Choose ideas together to form the middle of your story and write a sentence for the beginning and end. Make a large class book, illustrated and written by the children.	

Guided writing
Encourage correct use of capital letters and full stops. Ensure that spaces between words are accurate.

Assessment
Can children write sentences based on patterned language, words and phrases in familiar stories? Ask the children to complete the interactive assessment activity, 'The little gingerbread man' on the CD-ROM. Refer back to the learning outcomes on page 33.

Further work
Create themed storybooks, for example, about fantasy worlds, using the same sequence of activities.

My storyboard

◼ Write notes and draw pictures in this box about the beginning of your story.

◼ Write notes and draw pictures in this box about the middle of your story.

◼ Write notes and draw pictures in this box about the end of your story.

Rhyming words 1

mud	toes	bears
pairs	door	queue
snails	flood	tails
more	Balu	rows

NARRATIVE ■ UNIT 2

Rhyming words 2

cats	down	ark
teeth	flumps	dot
spot	dark	sneeth
humps	spats	town

Name _____ **Date** _____

Fantasy creatures

Illustrations © Nova Developments.

■ 100 LITERACY FRAMEWORK LESSONS YEAR 1

NARRATIVE
UNIT 3 Traditional and fairy tales

Speak and listen for a range of purposes on paper and on screen

Strand 1 Speaking
- Tell stories and incidents from their own experience in an audible voice.
- Retell stories, ordering events using story language.

Strand 2 Listening and responding
- Listen with sustained concentration, building new stores of words.
- Listen to tapes or video and express views about how a story has been presented.

Strand 3 Group discussion and interaction
- Take turns to speak, listen to others' suggestions and talk about what they are going to do.

Strand 4 Drama
- Explore familiar themes and characters through improvisation and role play.
- Act out their own and well-known stories, using voices for characters.

Read for a range of purposes on paper and on screen

Strand 5 Word recognition: decoding (reading) and encoding (spelling)
- Apply phonic knowledge and skills as the prime approach to reading and spelling unfamiliar words that are not completely decodable.

Strand 7 Understanding and interpreting texts
- Identify the main events and characters in stories.
- Make predictions showing an understanding of ideas, events and characters.
- Recognise the main elements that shape different texts.

Strand 8 Engaging with and responding to texts
- Select books for personal reading and give reasons for choices.
- Visualise and comment on events, characters and ideas, making imaginative links to their own experiences.

Write for a range of purposes on paper and on screen

Strand 9 Creating and shaping texts
- Independently choose what to write about, plan and follow it through.
- Use key features of narrative in their own writing.
- Find and use new and interesting words and phrases, including story language.
- Create short simple texts that combine words with images and sounds.

Strand 10 Text structure and organisation
- Group written sentences together in chunks of meaning or subject.

Strand 11 Sentence structure and punctuation
- Compose and write simple sentences independently to communicate meaning.
- Use capital letters and full stops when punctuating simple sentences.

Strand 12 Presentation
- Use the space bar and keyboard to type their name and simple texts.

Progression in narrative

In this year children are moving towards:
- Listening to and reading stories which provoke different responses; identifying the beginning, middle and end and making predictions; recognising main characters and typical characteristics; noticing how dialogue is presented.
- Retelling familiar stories and recounting events.

UNIT 3 Traditional and fairy tales *continued*

■ Using patterns and language from familiar stories in own writing.

Key aspects of learning covered in this Unit

Reasoning
Children will have opportunities to compare different versions of stories to express their opinions and make judgements about which they prefer.

Creative thinking
Children will respond imaginatively to character descriptions, exploring motives and behaviour through role play.

Empathy
Children will consider the thoughts, feelings and actions of characters in stories.

Social skills
Children will learn about taking turns, listening to others and trying to reach agreement as they work together in a group.

Communication
Children will develop their ability to speak for an audience as they tell stories for a group.

Evaluation
Children will listen to one another's oral and written stories and give feedback about specific aspects. They will have the chance to judge their own work and decide on areas that they would like to improve.

Prior learning

Before starting this Unit check that the children can:
■ Re-enact a story with events in the right order.
■ Use words and phrases or patterns from texts read when writing stories.
■ Write in complete sentences with capital letters and full stops.
If they need further support refer to a prior Unit or to the Foundation Stage.

Resources

Phase 1: *Little Red Riding Hood* (core and differentiated) by Jean Evans ✸; Photocopiable page 69 'Beginning, middle and end'; Photocopiable page 70 'Sequencing words'; *Three Billy Goats Gruff* by Jean Evans ✸; Photocopiable page 71 'Jumbled sentences'
Phase 2: *Little Red Riding Hood* (core and differentiated) by Jean Evans ✸; *Three Billy Goats Gruff* by Jean Evans ✸; Pictures of wolves, goats and trolls; Props relating to traditional tales in 'story bags'
Phase 3: Selection of 'Little Red Riding Hood' books; Photocopiable page 72 'Characters'; Large construction equipment; Goats' tabards; Troll mask
Phase 4: *We're going on a bear hunt* (book and DVD version) by Michael Rosen and Helen Oxenbury (Walker); *We're going on a bear hunt – extracts 1* and *2* ✸; Bear Hunt clip ✸; *Jack and the beanstalk* (book and CD version) by Richard Walker (Barefoot); 'Giant's castle' role-play area
Phase 5: *We're going on a bear hunt: Play* by Vivian French, Michael Rosen and Helen Oxenbury (Walker); *We're going on a bear hunt – extract 3* by Michael Rosen and Helen Oxenbury ✸; *We're going on a bear hunt (Story play) – extracts 1* and *2* ✸; Puppets or small-world characters
Phase 6: *Jack and the beanstalk – extracts 1, 2* and *3* by Richard Walker ✸; *Jack and the beanstalk* (differentiated) by Jean Evans ✸; Photograph of a beanstalk ✸

Cross-curricular opportunities

Science (Growing, Animals); Geography (Journeys); PSHE (Feelings)

UNIT 3 ■ Teaching sequence

Phase	Children's objectives	Summary of activities	Learning outcomes
1	I can retell a familiar traditional tale. I can retell a familiar tale using sequencing words and voice change. I can retell a familiar traditional tale by sorting jumbled sentences.	Tell the story of 'Little Red Riding Hood' to one another in small groups. Use sequencing words and voice change to support storytelling. Sequence sentences to retell the story of 'Three Billy Goats Gruff'. Retell a story of their choice using acquired skills .	Children can identify the main events in traditional tales, sequencing them in chronological order.
2	I can compare familiar traditional tales. I can use puppets and props to re-enact a story.	Compare stories 'Little Red Riding Hood' and 'Three Billy Goats Gruff' as class and two stories of their choice in pairs. Suggest ways of using given props to re-enact stories. Retell stories within groups and then to the class.	Children can retell a familiar story in chronological order using story language.
3	I can explore main characters in a familiar story. I can explore characters through role play. I can create a character profile.	Compare Little Red Riding Hood and the wolf in different versions of the story. Re-enact 'Three Billy Goats Gruff' to explore characters. Learn about creating written character profiles.	Children can discuss the appearance, behaviour, characteristics and goals of characters. Children can write a profile of a character using visual and written text.
4	I can attempt to read familiar phrases in a story. I can explore a different version of a story. I can compare two versions of the same story.	Read and join in with repeated phrases in *We're going on a bear hunt* and explore the emotions of characters in the story. Explore the DVD version of *We're going on a bear hunt* and make comparisons with the book. Compare the book and CD of *Jack and the beanstalk*.	Children can discuss how narratives on CD and DVD are presented and express an opinion about the different versions.
5	I can compare a book and play version of a story. I can explore a play version of a story. I can retell a story using puppets.	Compare pages of text from the book and play version of *We're Going on a Bear Hunt*. Read a play version of *We're going on a bear hunt* using different voices and expression for the characters. Use puppets to retell *We're Going on a Bear Hunt*.	Children can say what a playscript is for and can identify some ways in which it differs from a story text. Children can read a simple playscript aloud using appropriate expression.
6	I can retell a traditional story in my own words. I can develop and write a story plan with a partner. I can write my own version of a traditional story.	Retell a traditional story of their choosing. Write a story plan for 'Jack and the beanstalk'. Develop sequencing, characterisation and language for their story. Choose a traditional story and write their own version.	Children can write their own version of a traditional story, using a series of complete sentences organised into chronological order.

Provide copies of the objectives for the children.

DAY 1 ▪ Basic story elements

Key features	Stages	Additional opportunities
Empathy: considering the feelings of Red Riding Hood	**Introduction** Ask the children to recall the traditional story of 'Little Red Riding Hood'. Invite them to discuss characters and events as they remember them. Read the story to them using *Little Red Riding Hood* from the CD-ROM. Did they like or dislike any of the events? **Speaking and listening** Display photocopiable page 69 'Beginning, middle and end' and invite the children to say how the story starts. Write down words they use, including the story language, *Once upon a time*, under the heading *Beginning*. Make further notes about what happens in the middle and at the end of the story, using the children's language and any suitable story language.	**Support:** read the differentiated version of *Little Red Riding Hood* from the CD-ROM to small groups of children **Support:** explain how to make predictions from text as they join in such as *big eyes – better to see...*
Communication: speaking for an audience as they tell a story	**Independent work** Put the children into small groups and ask them to tell the story, firstly as individuals then as a group with a narrator and different character roles. Remind them to include events at the beginning, middle and end of the story.	
Evaluation: listening to one another's oral stories and giving feedback	**Plenary** Bring the class together and discuss how the children managed their storytelling. Did they find it easier to tell the story as a group, taking on parts and helping each other to remember events in sequence, or did they prefer to tell the story individually? Listen to examples of group and individual versions of the story and make comments as a class.	

DAY 2 ▪ Sequencing words and voice change

Key features	Stages	Additional opportunities
	Introduction Remind the children of their storytelling on Day 1 and explain that they are going to continue to develop their storytelling skills. **Speaking and listening** Read the *Little Red Riding Hood* extract from the CD-ROM again, drawing attention to predictable language by pausing for their response while you are reading, for example, *What big eyes you have! All the better to...you with.* Increase the volume of your voice as you reach the climax of the sequence, *Eat you with!* encouraging children to do the same as they join in.	**Phonics:** big, nose, smell, teeth, eat, ear, hear **HFW:** what, you, have, all, see, with, my, first, then, after, that, next, day **Support:** focus on the differentiated version of the story
Evaluation: commenting on specific aspects of the work of their partners	**Independent work** Put the children into pairs and supply each pair with a copy of photocopiable page 70, 'Sequencing words'. Ask them to cut out the boxes, arrange the sentences in order and use them to help them tell the story. Encourage them to remember the sequence of predictable dialogue and to vary their voices to match the character and level of tension in the story. Ask them to comment on each other's storytelling skills and suggest ways to develop them further.	**Extend:** use knowledge of phonics and HFW to read predictable language sequences and story language
Social skills: taking turns to speak and listen to others	**Plenary** Bring the class together and discuss the activity they completed in pairs. Listen to examples together and make comments. Create a collection of sequencing words and display them on a wall.	

DAY 3 ■ Retelling a familiar traditional tale by sorting jumbled sentences

Key features	Stages	Additional opportunities
	Introduction Ask the children to recall how they used sequencing, story language and voice variation to tell the story of 'Little Red Riding Hood'. Explain that you would like them to use these skills to retell another traditional tale.	**Phonics:** *trip-trap, billy, Gruff, big* **HFW:** three, little
	Speaking and listening Read *Three Billy Goats Gruff* from the CD-ROM, using voice variation for the characters and stressing patterned language. Ask questions to help children identify basic story elements and summarise the plot. Do they know who the main characters are? Can they describe the setting? What are the key events? What happens at the beginning, middle and end of the story?	
Communication: speaking to an audience **Evaluation:** listening to one another tell stories and making constructive suggestions for development	**Independent work** Put the children into pairs and ask them to retell the story. Give each pair a copy of photocopiable page 71 'Jumbled sentences', and read the sentences as a class. Does the story make sense? Why not? Ask the children to cut out the sentences, rearrange them in the correct order and take turns to tell the story to their partner using the sentences to help. Encourage them to vary their voices and to emphasise repeated phrases such as *Trip-trap, trip-trap.*	**Support:** work with an adult focusing on a printed copy of the CD-ROM story **Extend:** read a printed version of the CD-ROM story, using knowledge of phonics and HFW
	Plenary Bring the class together and ask individuals to tell the story while the others listen. Invite the others to make comments, for example, about the sequence of events and characters' voices, and suggestions for development of the story.	

DAY 4 ■ Retelling a familiar traditional tale using acquired skills

Key features	Stages	Additional opportunities
	Introduction Ask the children to recall the stories they have been telling one another on Days 1 to 3. Remind them about how they noted what happened at the beginning, middle and end of the story, and how they used story language in sentences to show this sequence. Discuss how they made the story more interesting by using different voices for characters and changing voice volume Ask the children to think of other stories they know well and make a list. Add some appropriate titles of your own if the children have difficulty with this.	**Extend:** compile lists in small groups
Creative thinking: responding imaginatively to character descriptions	**Independent work** Put the children into the pairs they have worked in before and ask each pair to choose a story from the list to tell to the others. Provide them with photocopiable page 69 'Beginning, middle and end'. Remind them to note down the sequence of events, referring to your wall display for sequencing words to use, to identify the main characters and make up voices for them, and to think of any patterned or predictable language in the story.	**Support:** work with a small group of children on retelling a very familiar story such as 'Goldilocks'
Evaluation: giving feedback on their own work and that of others	**Plenary** Bring the class together and choose examples of a selection of stories to listen to and discuss. How do the children feel they have managed the activity?	

Guided reading

To challenge children in guided reading, encourage them read the story sheets, using their acquired phonic knowledge and skills, along with automatic recognition of high frequency words. Use the differentiated version of *Little Red Riding Hood* from the CD-ROM for children who need support.

Assessment

Can children identify the main events in a traditional tale and sequence events using the headings *Beginning, Middle, End*?
Refer back to the learning outcomes on page 55.

Further work

Form self-assessment groups . Ask individuals to tell stories to one another and then discuss whether their objectives have been met successfully. Encourage them to suggest ways of developing skills.

DAY 1 ■ Comparing familiar traditional tales

Key features	Stages	Additional opportunities
	Introduction Read *Little Red Riding Hood* and *Three Billy Goats Gruff* from the CD-ROM to the children, if possible displaying each one as you read so that they can follow the text. Explain that you are going to discuss similarities and differences in the two stories.	**Support:** use the differentiated version of *Little Red Riding Hood* from the CD-ROM
Empathy: considering the thoughts, feelings and actions of characters	**Speaking and listening** Talk about the characters in the stories. Find pictures of wolves, goats and trolls and look at them together. Ask: *What are the differences between the wolf and goats in the stories and real animals? Is a troll a real or imaginary creature? Are there people in the stories? How might the characters be feeling?* Examine the story language used, pointing out the shared opening phrase *Once upon a time* and the satisfying end to each story. Discuss how lines are repeated in each story, changing by one or two words each time.	**Extend:** read the texts together before discussion
	Independent work Put the children into pairs and ask them to choose a different traditional story each to focus on. They can refer to the list made in Phase 1, Day 4 for examples. Ask them to discuss similarities and differences between their two chosen stories. Encourage them to talk about types of character, story language and endings.	
Social skills: listening to one another and taking turns to speak	**Plenary** Bring the class together and ask pairs of children to report back on their discussions. What are the differences and similarities?	

DAY 2 ■ Working with puppets and props

Key features	Stages	Additional opportunities
	Introduction Tell the children that they are going to play a game called 'Guess the story' and explain the simple rules. They will work in groups and be given a bag of props relating to a familiar traditional story. They will have to identify the story and then use the props to tell the story to the other children.	
	Speaking and listening Hold up an object that could be used as a prop in more than one story, for example, a wolf puppet, a small world cow or a stick puppet of an old man. Ask about how the prop might be used along with a selection of different props from a collection to tell two different stories. Open a story bag, for example, 'Goldilocks', and hold up the objects inside one by one. Ask the children to guess the story and talk about how they could use the props, such as three bowls, spoons and teddy bears.	
Social skills: working as a group to reach agreement about using the props effectively	**Independent work** Put the children into small groups and ask them to choose a story bag each. Allow time for them to explore the contents of the bag and decide which traditional story to re-enact and how to use the objects effectively.	**Extend:** provide children with a wider selection of props to choose from
Communication: speaking for an audience as they re-enact their stories	**Plenary** Bring the class together so that the groups can re-enact their stories with the props. Encourage comments on beginnings and endings, story language, characters and plots. Could these be improved?	**Support:** supply specific character puppets and objects related to the story

DAY 3 ■ Retelling of stories in groups using props

Key features	Stages	Additional opportunities
	Introduction Ask the children to recall a favourite story and identify whether the characters were good or bad. Make a list of storybook characters and then decide whether they are good or bad characters. Is it important to have both in a story?	**Phonics:** upon, end **HFW:** once, time, there, said, little, then, first, next, after
	Speaking and listening Display *Little Red Riding Hood* from the CD-ROM and invite the children to read it with you. Highlight any repeated story language. Do the same with *Three Billy Goats Gruff* from the CD-ROM. Identify any common story language in the texts, such as *Once upon a time*, and write these on a large sheet of paper. Invite the children to suggest other familiar story phrases such as *happily ever after*.	**Support:** use the differentiated version of *Little Red Riding Hood*
Creative thinking: responding to characters through role play	**Independent work** Put the children into groups, each with a box of different types of props relating to a story, for example, boxes of small world equipment, puppets, dressing-up clothes, everyday objects, soft toys. Include the story text and allow time for children to retell the story within the group using their given category of props.	**Extend:** read the texts and highlight repeated language themselves
Evaluation: listening to oral re-enactment of stories and giving feedback about specific aspects	**Plenary** Bring the class together and have the groups take turns to retell their stories using their props. Which type of prop was most effective? Did the children retell the story in correct sequence? Did they use appropriate language? Could the stories have been developed further? Can they suggest how?	

Guided reading
Read *Little Red Riding Hood* and *Three Billy Goats Gruff* from the CD-ROM and encourage them to highlight story language and repeated phrases. Invite them to identify the main characters and events and find specific information.

Assessment
Can children retell a traditional tale in their own words for a group of children?
Do they speak audibly and use some story language?
Refer back to the learning outcomes on page 55.

Further work
Leave story bags and various props in the book corner and encourage children to use them to retell stories to one another when they visit.

DAY 1 ■ Exploring characters

Key features	Stages	Additional opportunities
	Introduction Ask the children to recall the story of 'Little Red Riding Hood'. Who are the characters in the story? Explain that they are going to discuss the main characters in more detail and decide how they might look, speak and behave.	**Phonics:** red, hood, woodcutter, granny **HFW:** little
Empathy: considering the thoughts, feelings and actions of characters	**Speaking and listening** Show the children a selection of books about Little Red Riding Hood and invite them to choose two for you to read aloud. Talk about how Little Red Riding Hood was portrayed. For example: *Did she look the same in each book? Was there any difference in what she said? Did she react in the same way to the things that happened to her?* Do the same for the wolf in each story.	**Support:** look at illustrations and comment on characters' appearance
Social skills: taking turns and listening and trying to reach agreement	**Independent work** Put the children into small groups and ask each group to choose one of the books to look at. Provide each group with photocopiable page 72 'Characters'. Ask the children to discuss how Little Red Riding Hood looks, what she says and how she reacts to events, and to make notes in the appropriate columns. Ask them to do the same with the wolf. Is it easy to tell which is the good and which is the bad character by the things that they say?	**Extend:** visualise and comment on characters by referring to text and illustrations
Communication: speaking for an audience as they present their findings	**Plenary** Bring the groups together to present their findings to the others. Make comparisons about how the characters are represented in the stories.	

DAY 2 ■ Exploring *Three Billy Goats Gruff* characters through role play

Key features	Stages	Additional opportunities
	Introduction Before the lesson create a bridge from large construction equipment in the hall or outdoor area. Leave three simple goats' tabards made from brown fabric and a troll mask alongside. Bring the children to the area and ask them to sit in a large circle to recall the 'Three Billy Goats Gruff' story. Who are the characters? Who is the bad character?	
	Speaking and listening Show the children several versions of the story and ask someone to choose one for you to read aloud. Read it and invite the children to join in with familiar dialogue, using different voices for each character. Suggest that they discover more about the characters by re-enacting the story in groups of five.	**Extend:** make predictions about how a character might behave in different situations
Empathy: understanding more about how the characters are feeling	**Independent work** Ask the children to find a clear space to work in. Talk about the need for a narrator to tell the story and children to take on the roles of the troll and billy goats. Ask them to think about how the characters feel, how they will move, what they will say and the voices they will use.	**Support:** link the goats' fear of the troll to their own experiences of being frightened
Creative thinking: exploring characters' motives and behaviour through role play	**Plenary** Bring the children together and ask them to sit facing the bridge you have created. Choose groups to re-enact the story using the props. Discuss their interpretations. Are there similarities and differences? How effective is the chosen dialogue? Do children feel they understand the characters more now?	

DAY 3 Creating a character profile

Key features	Stages	Additional opportunities
	## Introduction Invite the children to recall the activities relating to storybook characters on Days 1 and 2 and tell them that you would like them to choose a favourite character to write a profile about. Explain what the lesson will involve and ask questions to ensure that the children understand the meaning of 'character profile'. ## Speaking and listening Remind the children of how they explored characters by looking at books, discussing how they might look, react and speak, and by taking on different roles. Choose a popular character and demonstrate how to write a profile, with the children contributing with their own ideas. Include an illustration and annotate it with captions and labels.	
Creative thinking: responding with imaginative ideas **Social skills:** discussing and sharing ideas **Communication:** speaking for an audience	## Independent work Put the children into pairs and ask individuals to choose a character to profile. Encourage them to use different ways of representing different aspects of the character, for example, with a labelled illustration or short sentence, and to include any repeated phrases used by the character. Encourage them to discuss their ideas with their partners. ## Plenary Bring the children together again and invite them to take turns to talk about their character profiles. Encourage others to ask questions about them.	**Support:** write single descriptive words under their drawings **Extend:** include appropriate sentences of dialogue for their chosen characters

Guided reading and writing
Make lists of appropriate words to support children as they compile lists of characteristics and write profiles. Encourage children to apply their phonic knowledge and skills as the prime approach to reading and spelling unfamiliar words that are not completely decodable.

Assessment
Can children describe the behaviour, appearance and characteristics of a particular character in talk, pictures and written captions?
Refer back to the learning outcomes on page 55.

Further work
Invite children to take on some of the good and bad character roles explored on Days 1 to 3 and let others question them about their behaviour, motives and goals.

DAY 1 ■ Exploring story characters

Key features	Stages	Additional opportunities
	Introduction Read *We're going on a bear hunt* to the children and talk about the story settings and events. What did the children like about the story? Was there anything they disliked? How did it make them feel?	
	Speaking and listening Display *We're going on a bear hunt– extract 1* from the CD-ROM. Look at the characters shown and compare their appearances. Do the children think they are from one family? Who might the adult be? Why is the baby being carried? Display *We're going on a bear hunt– extract 2* showing the characters about to cross the river. Invite the children to discuss the rhythm and repetition of words and to read them aloud. Look for this sequence of patterned language on other pages.	**Support:** point to the text as they repeat phrases **Extend:** read unfamiliar two-syllable words by identifying the constituent parts
Social skills: taking turns to share their opinions **Empathy:** considering the thoughts, feelings and actions of the characters	**Independent work** Put the children into pairs and ask them to consider how the characters are feeling at different points in the story. How can they tell? Encourage them to discuss the emotions the characters experience, such as happiness, excitement, worry and fear. Ask them to choose a character, draw a picture of his/her reaction to an event and write a sentence about it. Suggest that they explain their picture and read their sentence to their partner.	
	Plenary Bring the children together and invite one child from each pair to show their partner's picture, talk about it and read the sentence.	

DAY 2 ■ A story on DVD

Key features	Stages	Additional opportunities
	Introduction Read *We're going on a bear hunt* again and ask the children to recall their explorations into characters, settings and events. Explain that they are going to watch a DVD of the story to see what is the same and what is different.	**Phonics:** hunt, catch, big, not, under, got **HFW:** go, going, one, can't, over, have
Reasoning: comparing different versions of a story and expressing opinions about which they prefer	**Speaking and listening** Play the Bear Hunt video clip from the CD-ROM to the children and then ask what they liked or disliked about it. If possible play the entire DVD. Ask: *How was it different from the book version? Which version did you prefer?* Encourage the children to consider the DVD background music, the changing voices of the narrators and the additional sounds, such as birds singing and ducks quacking. Did these effects create more excitement? Discuss how the movement of the characters was presented, for example, the girl tip-toeing lightly in time to a rhythmic double bass. Explain the meaning of *animation*.	
	Independent work Put the children into small groups and supply each group with a large sheet of paper divided into two columns headed *Same* and *Different*. Ask them to use these columns to note similarities and differences between the book and DVD.	**Support:** write simple words using phonics as the prime approach to spelling
Social skills: taking turns to express own ideas and listening to others express theirs	**Plenary** Bring the children together and invite groups to take turns to present their findings. Which was the most popular version? Read and watch the two versions again in the light of explorations. Have the children anything to add?	**Extend:** attempt to spell more complex words by segmenting sounds

DAY 3 ■ Exploring two versions of a story

Key features	Stages	Additional opportunities
	Introduction Invite the children to recall the results of their comparisons between a book and DVD version of the same story and explain that they are going to do the same with a book and CD version of 'Jack and the beanstalk'.	
	Speaking and listening Play the CD version of the story and invite the children to listen to it. Discuss the tape, for example: *Was it easy to imagine the characters, settings and events without having the illustrations in a book to look at? Were there any sound effects to add atmosphere? Did the narrator make the characters come to life by changing his voice?*	
Creative thinking: responding imaginatively to spoken character descriptions **Reasoning:** expressing opinions on written and CD versions of a story and making judgements on which they prefer	**Independent work** Put the children into pairs to talk about the story they have just heard on the CD. Invite them each to choose a character from the story and draw a picture of this character using only their memory of listening to the CD to help. Next, ask the children to listen while you read the book version of the story, showing them the illustrations and making up voices for the characters. Did they find this version helped them to imagine the characters differently? Give the children time to add more detail to their pictures. **Plenary** Bring the children together to share their pictures. Which story did they prefer? In what ways could the CD version be improved? Create a role-play giant's castle so that the children can re-enact story scenes in later activity time.	**Support:** scribe words related to the children's pictures **Extend:** use developing awareness of word structure and spelling to write a sentence about their chosen character under their picture

Guided reading and writing
Encourage word recognition by asking children to help read the chosen texts and spell their related sentences.
Draw attention to familiar high frequency words as they occur.

Assessment
Can the children listen attentively to a story on CD and talk about how it has been presented?
Refer back to the learning outcomes on page 55.

Further work
Challenge the children to compare a wider range of versions of the same story, such as video films, musical versions, CD and DVD.

DAY 1 ▪ Comparing texts

Key features	Stages	Additional opportunities
	Introduction Ask the children to recall the story of *We're going on a bear hunt*. What can they remember about the book and DVD version? Tell them that they are going to begin to explore a play version of the story and compare this with the book.	**Phonics:** hunt, catch, not, big, uh-uh, river, deep, under **HFW:** go, going, one, what, day, can't, over, no
Reasoning: reading book and play versions of a story and making judgements about text	**Speaking and listening** Display *We're going on a bear hunt– extract 3* from the CD-ROM and read the words together. Draw attention to the catchphrases and repetition and explain that these make the story easier to read. Now display *We're going a bear hunt (Story play) – extract 1* and *extract 2* and explain that the coloured lines show which character is speaking. Ask the children to read them. Did they find this easy? Were there any catchphrases or repeated language to help?	
Creative thinking: responding imaginatively to character dialogue	**Independent work** Put the children into small groups and supply them with copies of the story play extracts. Ask them to try reading the lines and deciding who the characters are. Invite them to experiment with different voices.	
Evaluation: judging aspects of pages of text from book and play and give preferences	**Plenary** Bring the class together, still sitting in their groups, and ask them to explain whether they enjoyed the play or book extracts most. Do the children think the play will be more interesting than the book, perhaps more difficult to read but more exciting and fun to act. Do they think they will find out more about the characters with the extra dialogue?	

DAY 2 ▪ We're going on a bear hunt - the play

Key features	Stages	Additional opportunities
	Introduction Discuss the children's conclusions from explorations of pages from the book and play versions of *We're going on a bear hunt* on Day 1 and explain that they will be developing their ideas further as they explore the whole play.	
	Speaking and listening Show the children the play version and ask questions about how the story might be told. Explain that plays are dramatic versions of stories with people taking on the roles of the different characters. Read the whole play to the children, changing your voice for the different characters. Choose children who are able to read the different parts and invite them to 'tell the story' to the others. Read the book version to the children and make comparisons between the two ways of telling the story. Invite them to join in as you read each version. Discuss how joining in with the play is more difficult because the language is no longer predictable.	
Social skills: learning about taking turns, listening to others and reaching a group agreement	**Independent work** Put the children into groups of four, providing each with a copy of *We're going on a bear hunt (Story play) – extracts 1* and *2*. Ask them to practise reading their parts, each reading a given coloured line. Encourage discussion about adapting voices, and adding atmosphere with tone and volume.	**Support:** join in with familiar language
Evaluation: giving feedback about their different interpretations of the play	**Plenary** Invite groups to take turns to read the extracts. Discuss the way characters have been portrayed and explore modifying voices for effect.	**Extend:** read the whole play using acquired word recognition skills

DAY 3 ■ Using puppets to retell a story

Key features	Stages	Additional opportunities
	### Introduction Ask the children what they have learned from reading the book and play versions of *We're going on a bear hunt* and watching the DVD. Explain that they will be using this knowledge, along with props, to help them to retell the story.	**HFW:** big, little, dad, dog, man, girl, sister, boy, brother
	### Speaking and listening Invite the children to make a list of the five characters in the story. Discuss the ways that these characters could be represented, for example, using finger, stick or hand puppets, or small-world characters. Emphasise the need to consider the dialogue, repetitive language and catchphrases they might include and the importance of noting the events in sequence. Display *We're going on a bear hunt– extract 4* from the CD-ROM depicting the sequence of events and explain that you will leave this on display for the children to refer to.	
Creative thinking: using puppets imaginatively, making up appropriate dialogue	### Independent work Put the children into groups and supply each group with a set of puppets or small-world characters to work with. Encourage them to decide upon who will operate each character and make up appropriate dialogue, and which lines will be said by all of the characters. Refer them to the display to sequence events.	**Support:** scribe unfamiliar words suggested by children
Evaluation: judging their work and the work of others and discuss areas for improvement.	### Plenary Bring the children together to take turns to retell the story with their puppets. Discuss which versions are most effective and why, and suggest improvements.	

Guided writing
Ask children to write their own list of characters using their knowledge of HFW. Encourage children to identify the constituent parts of two-syllable and three-syllable words such as *today* and *umbrella* to support application of phonic knowledge and skills.

Assessment
Can children read a playscript, adapting their voices for different characters?
Refer back to the learning outcomes on page 55.

Further work
Supply further play scripts at the appropriate reading level for children to read together. Provide them with facilities to record themselves to play back to others

DAY 1 ■ Retelling a traditional story

Key features	Stages	Additional opportunities
	Introduction Ask the children to recall the story of 'Jack and the beanstalk' and explain that they are going to work in pairs to retell another story in their own words.	**Phonics:** lazy, saying, offing, just, lived, cow **HFW:** that, was, when, there, time, little, way, out, very, much
	Speaking and listening Invite the children to choose a favourite story and describe what happens at the beginning, middle and end. Display *Jack and the beanstalk – extract 1* from the CD-ROM and read the text aloud. How do the words set the scene? Is the main character introduced? Are there any repeated phrases that might appear again? Display and read *Jack and the beanstalk – extract 2* beginning with the words *FEE, FI, FO, FUM* and ask the children to describe what is happening. How is the other main character, introduced on this page, portrayed? Display and read *Jack and the beanstalk – extract 3*. Talk about how the author draws the story to a satisfying close by describing what all the characters are doing.	**Support:** use the differentiated version of *Jack and the beanstalk* from the CD-ROM
Social skills: taking turns to speak and listen to one another	**Independent work** Put the children into pairs and invite each pair to choose a story to retell. Ask them to talk about what happens at the beginning, middle and end of the story, and any significant events, and then try to retell the story in correct sequence.	**Extend:** make notes about the beginning, middle and end of their chosen story
Communication: speaking for an audience as they retell their chosen stories	**Plenary** Bring the class together and invite some of them to take turns to retell their chosen stories. Discuss if each story had a clear beginning and end, introduced events in the correct sequence and used words from the original version.	

DAY 2 ■ Writing a story plan with a partner

Key features	Stages	Additional opportunities
	Introduction Show the children the picture of a beanstalk growing from the CD-ROM. Which story does it remind them of? What event led up to the beanstalk starting to grow? What event followed the beanstalk reaching full height? Tell them that they will need to put events into the correct order when they write their own stories.	
	Speaking and listening Ask the children to help you to create a story plan and display photocopiable page 69 'Beginning, middle and end'. Refer to *Jack and the beanstalk – extract 1* from the CD-ROM and ask the children to suggest brief notes to write about the beginning of the story. Read extracts 2 and 3 together to remind the children of what happens.	**Support:** refer to the differentiated version of *Jack and the beanstalk* from the CD-ROM
	Independent work Put the children into pairs and supply each pair with photocopiable page 69. Ask the children to write notes about the middle of the story then come to a class decision about what to write on the main display. Do the same with the end of the story.	
Evaluation: judging their own work and deciding upon areas to improve	**Plenary** Bring the class together to read out the group notes they have made. Are they satisfied with their efforts? Do they think they will be able to write the main events of the story in the correct sequence using their notes?	

DAY 3 ■ Developing the story with a partner

Key features	Stages	Additional opportunities
	Introduction Display the class notes made on Day 2. Do the children think that they will be sufficient to help them to write their own version of the story? On a large sheet of paper write an opening sentence to the story, similar to the original and including the catchphrase *a little bit of this and a little bit of that*. Read what you have written and ask the children for ways of improving it.	**HFW:** little, this, and, that
Social skills: working as a class to develop ideas	**Independent work** Put the children into pairs and ask them to discuss how to tell the next significant event in the story and then write this down. Choose one of the pairs to read out their event and add this to the class story. Continue with the next event, choosing the work of another pair, until the story is complete.	
Evaluation: considering their joint effort and suggesting modifications	**Plenary** Bring the class together and read the story to them. Are they satisfied with it? Have they included appropriate story language and mentioned all events?	

DAY 4 ■ Writing the whole story

Key features	Stages	Additional opportunities
	Introduction Talk to the children about how they created a class version of 'Jack and the beanstalk' on Day 3 and invite them to use the same approach to write their own versions of favourite traditional stories. Supply a list of titles to choose from.	
	Speaking and listening Remind the children to start by writing notes about the beginning, middle and end of the story and then to compose sentences for each section. Emphasise the importance of catchphrases and story language such as *Once upon a time*.	**Support:** some children may prefer to type texts on a keyboard
Evaluation: giving feedback about aspects of written stories	**Independent work** Suggest that the children work with partners so that they can share their stories. Encourage them to help one another to modify their stories until they are satisfied.	
Communication: speaking for an audience	**Plenary** Bring the class together and invite individuals to read their stories. Encourage positive comments about individual efforts. Display the finished stories.	

Guided reading
Cover key objectives when children read texts together, for example, encourage them to identify constituent parts of two-syllable and three-syllable words. Identify and highlight high frequency words on the displayed texts.

Assessment
Can children write their own version of a traditional story with events organised into beginning, middle and end, using complete sentences? Ask them to complete the CD-ROM assessment activity, reading the play version of 'Little Red Riding Hood'. Refer back to the learning outcomes on page 55.

Further work
Extend opportunities to type stories on a keyboard and encourage children to create their own storybooks by illustrating their typed pages.

Beginning, middle and end

Beginning

Middle

End

Sequencing words

■ Cut out the extracts and put them in the correct order.

✂

After that the big bad wolf tried to eat her.
Next she skipped along the path.
At the end they all had a cup of tea.
Once upon a time there was a little girl.
Then she saw a big bad wolf.
First she walked down the path into the wood.
At last the woodcutter chased the wolf away.

PHOTOCOPIABLE ■ SCHOLASTIC
www.scholastic.co.uk

Jumbled sentences

■ Cut out the extracts and put them in the correct order.

✂

He landed in the water and that was the end of the troll.

One by one the billy goats went to cross the bridge.

The big billy goat bent his head and hit the troll.

Once upon a time there lived three billy goats called Gruff.

So the three billy goats lived happily ever after eating sweet grass.

First went the little billy goat, trip, trap, trip trap.

Last went the big billy goat, trip, trip, BANG, BANG.

Out popped the troll.

Next went the middle-sized billy goat, trip, trap, trip, trap.

Characters

	Red Riding Hood	Wolf
Appearance		
Language		
Behaviour		

NARRATIVE
UNIT 4 Stories about fantasy worlds

Speak and listen for a range of purposes on paper and on screen

Strand 4 Drama
■ Explore familiar themes and characters through improvisation and role play.

Read for a range of purposes on paper and on screen

Strand 5 Word recognition: decoding (reading) and encoding (spelling)
■ Apply phonic knowledge and skills as the prime approach to reading and spelling unfamiliar words that are not completely decodable.
■ Read more challenging texts, which can be decoded using their acquired phonic knowledge and skills, along with automatic recognition of high frequency words.
■ Read and spell phonically decodable two-syllable and three-syllable words.
Strand 6 Word structure and spelling
■ Spell new words using phonics as the prime approach.
■ Segment sounds into their constituent phonemes in order to spell them correctly.
■ Recognise and use alternative ways of spelling graphemes already taught.
■ Use knowledge of common inflections in spelling, such as plurals, -ly, -er.
■ Read and spell phonically decodable two-syllable and three-syllable words.
Strand 7 Understanding and interpreting texts
■ Use syntax and context when reading for meaning.
■ Recognise the main elements that shape different texts.

Write for a range of purposes on paper and on screen

Strand 9 Creating and shaping texts
■ Use key features of narrative in their own writing.
■ Create short simple texts on paper and on screen that combine words with images (and sounds).
Strand 11 Sentence structure and punctuation
■ Compose and write simple sentences independently to communicate meaning.
■ Use capital letters and full stops when punctuating simple sentences.
Strand 12 Presentation
■ Use the space bar and keyboard to type their name and simple texts.

Progression in narrative

In this year, children are moving towards:
■ Listening to and reading a range of stories on page and screen which provoke different responses: identifying the beginning, middle and end in stories and using familiarity with this structure to make predictions about endings; recalling the main events.
■ Identifying the goals or motives of characters and talking about how they move the plot on; beginning to use different voices for particular characters.
■ Creating stories orally, on page and screen, that will impact on listeners and readers in a range of ways.
■ Using patterns and language from familiar stories in own writing; writing complete stories using developing sentence structure and punctuation skills; planning stories with a beginning – middle – end, decide where they are set and use ideas from reading for some incidents and events.

UNIT 4 ◄ Stories about fantasy worlds *continued*

Key aspects of learning covered in this Unit

Problem solving
Children will identify problems and resolutions for a main character, applying their prior experience of adventure narratives to consider a range of possible solutions.

Creative thinking
Children will generate imaginative ideas in response to visual stimuli and make connections through play.

Reasoning
Children will predict events in a text, expressing and justifying their opinions based on evidence from the text and prior experience.

Evaluation
Children will discuss success criteria for their work, give feedback to others and judge the effectiveness of their own writing.

Empathy
Children will consider the thoughts, feelings and actions of characters in stories.

Social skills
When developing collaborative writing, children will learn about listening to and respecting other people's ideas.

Communication
Children will develop their ability to discuss as they work collaboratively in paired, group and whole-class contexts. They will communicate outcomes orally, in writing and through ICT.

Prior learning

Before starting this Unit check that the children can:
- Offer opinions about a specific author's work.
- Understand the concept of a simple sentence.
If they need further support refer to a prior Unit or to the Foundation Stage.

Resources

Phase 1: *Here come the aliens!* by Colin McNaughton (Walker); *Here come the aliens! – extract 1* ✎; *The kiss that missed – extract 1* ✎; Picture of an undersea landscape ✎; *Room on the Broom* by Julia Donaldson (Macmillan); *The kiss that missed – extract 2* ✎; *The Smartest Giant in Town* by Julia Donaldson (Macmillan); Picture of a fairy castle ✎;

Phase 2: *The kiss that missed* by David Melling (Hodder); *The kiss that missed – extract 2* ✎; A musical triangle; Photocopiable page 90 'Describe the moods'; Photocopiable page 91 'Solve the problem'; Props for storytelling

Phase 3: Picture of an undersea landscape ✎; *The kiss that missed – extract 2* ✎; *Here come the aliens! – extract 1* ✎; Spooky music; A poster of children involved in an activity; Photocopiable page 49 'My storyboard'; Photocopiable page 92 'Compose a sentence'; Puppets; Dressing-up clothes; Small-world characters; Story bags; Assessment activity 'Writing stories' ✎

Cross-curricular opportunities

Geography (under the sea, forests, jungles, space)
History (stories set in the past)

UNIT 4 ■ Teaching sequence

Phase	Children's objectives	Summary of activities	Learning outcomes
1	I can compare fantasy worlds. / I can explore images of fantasy worlds. / I can identify how objects in fantasy worlds differ. / I can follow a character's adventure in a fantasy setting. / I can create a fantasy setting. / I can explore aspects of a fantasy story. / I can predict possible events in a narrative through role play.	Compare outer space and fairy tale castle settings through two stories. Choose a fantasy world and describe setting and characters. Search books for objects which identify the setting. Read *The Smartest Giant in Town* and make up their own fantasy land. Use a range of creative and graphic resources to create castles. Create their own mobile spaceship to transport an alien. Go for an imaginary walk in a fantasy setting and predict events.	Children can predict possible events in a narrative based on their experiences of other texts.
2	I can explore a character's reactions to an event. / I can decide upon settings and characters for an adventure story. / I can introduce a problem and resolution into a narrative. / I can retell a whole class narrative orally with events organised sequentially. / I can retell own narrative orally.	Adopt the stances of characters from *The kiss that missed*. Choose an appropriate setting and photograph themselves adopting character poses. Work in pairs and as a class to compose a suitable problem and resolution for their story. Follow the sequence of their whole class narrative as they retell it orally. Retell their own narratives.	Children can orally tell an adventure narrative during role play with the events organised sequentially into problem and resolution.
3	I can explore a fantasy setting through role play. / I can identify a problem and resolution for a character. / I can plan a story with beginning, middle and end. / I can create visual images for a narrative. / I can develop sentence structure and punctuation skills. / I can write sentences that convey meaning and have correct punctuation. / I can plan an individual storybook. / I can write an individual story with events organised sequentially.	Pretend to walk through a chosen fantasy setting. Consider possible problems for their main character. Decide collaboratively on sentences for the beginning, middle and end of their class story. Decide appropriate visual presentation of ideas on the pages of their book. Practise composing sentences that convey meaning and include a capital letter and a full stop. Write joint sentences related to the images in their book. Use a wide range of resources to plan out a story idea. Write stories with events organised sequentially.	Children can compose complete sentences correctly demarcated by capital letters and full stops. / Children can write a story with the events organised sequentially into problem and resolution.

Provide copies of the objectives for the children.

DAY 1 ■ Comparing fantasy worlds

Key features	Stages	Additional opportunities
	Introduction Establish that children understand the meaning of the words 'real' and 'fantasy' and explain that they are going to explore some stories set in fantasy worlds. Display *Here come the aliens! – extract 1* from the CD-ROM, showing the unusual planets. Read the accompanying text. Where might the story be set?	**Phonics:** pl*a*net, c*a*stle, tw*i*nkle, bedr*oo*m, r*o*yal
	Speaking and listening Read *Here come the aliens!* and discuss the appearance and behaviour of the aliens. Are the creatures real or fantasy? Display *The kiss that missed – extract 1* from the CD-ROM, showing the prince in bed. Where might this story be set? Read the story and make comments about differences between the two stories.	
Communication: working collaboratively to choose appropriate words to annotate pictures	**Independent work** Put the children into pairs and invite them to choose an outer space or fairy tale castle setting and draw a picture about. Ask them to discuss their pictures with their partners and to decide upon appropriate words to annotate them. Annotate *The kiss that missed – extract 1* to demonstrate how to do this.	
Social skills: listening and respect other people's ideas **Evaluation:** giving feedback to others	**Plenary** Bring the children together and have a blank screen or large sheet of paper divided into two columns ready to make lists of their words. Begin by asking those who have drawn an outer space scene to show their pictures and read their words. Choose words to write on the screen as a class. Do the same with the castle pictures. Contrast the settings, using the lists to support suggestions.	

DAY 2 ■ Exploring images of fantasy settings

Key features	Stages	Additional opportunities
	Introduction Remind the children of their comparisons between outer space and fairy tale settings. Did they have a preference for one of the settings? Can they say why?	
	Speaking and listening Display a photograph of a lunar landscape and ask the children to describe it Do they think this landscape is real or fantasy? Talk about creatures who might live here, perhaps aliens similar to the ones in the story they have read. Display the photograph of an undersea landscape from the CD-ROM. Encourage comments about how the image makes the children feel and the characters who might live there. Can they predict possible events that might happen? Have they discovered any other fantasy settings in stories they have heard or films they have seen?	
Communication: deciding upon appropriate words together, commenting on each other's ideas and making effective changes	**Independent work** Put the children into pairs to discuss the fantasy worlds the class have explored. Invite them to choose one of these, or any imaginary world that they are both familiar with, and write down some words to describe it. Ask them to write down words naming and/or describing the characters who might live there.	**Support:** spell words with adult support **Extend:** spell words independently using their phonic knowledge and skills and awareness of HFW
Evaluation: giving feedback on ideas	**Plenary** Bring the children together and invite pairs to describe their fantasy settings and the characters who inhabit them, using their words to support them. Encourage others to comment on the ideas. Which ones would make the most exciting stories? Save the lists made by the children for future work.	

DAY 3 ■ Searching for objects in a fantasy world

Key features	Stages	Additional opportunities
Social skills: listening to one another and taking turns to speak	### Introduction Remind the children of the fantasy stories they have heard and the settings they have explored. In what ways are they different from one another and from the children's everyday world? Discuss this. ### Speaking and listening Read a fantasy story such as *Room on the Broom* and then look for similarities and differences between the witch's world and the children's world. Examine each page for objects that identify this world, for example, a cauldron, witch's hat, magic broomstick, wand and dragon. Discuss the sequence of events. Display *The kiss that missed – extract 2* from the CD-ROM and ask the children to identify objects that are different from their own world. Annotate the resource with labels such as armour, shield, and knight.	**Extend:** invite children to write the words on the display reminding them of key objectives for encoding
Communication: working collaboratively to compile group lists	### Independent work Put the children into pairs and provide each pair with photocopiable page 88 'In the witch's cave'. Ask them to recall the activity for *Room on the Broom* and then put a ring round objects related to the witch's world. Ask them to make a list of the objects they have circled. Encourage discussion about how objects differ from things they might find in their own homes or in other story settings. ### Plenary Bring the class together and invite them to take turns to read out their lists. Are the words the same or have some pairs listed different objects? Discuss reasons for choosing the objects. Keep the children's lists for later use.	**Support:** encourage less confident children to encode words, supporting them with specific objectives as appropriate

DAY 4 ■ Adventure in a fantasy setting

Key features	Stages	Additional opportunities
	### Introduction Ask the children to identify some of the ways in which the fantasy worlds they have explored have differed. Explain that you are going to read another story and you want them to be looking out for and remembering unusual things.	**Phonics:** *George, giant, gown, giraffe, goat*
Empathy: considering the thoughts and feelings of the giant	### Speaking and listening Read a story such as *The Smartest Giant in Town* which features fantasy or fairy tale characters. Identify the main character and discuss them. For example: What makes George, the giant, different? How does he feel about being so big? Ask them to find characters from other fairy tales such as dwarfs, little pigs and billy goats. Discuss how the author has invented a land full of story characters.	
Creative thinking: children create imaginary lands inspired by the story they have heard	### Independent work Put the children into pairs and ask them to invent a similar land, choosing their favourite storybook characters to live there. Who will be the main character? What might happen to him/her? Encourage the children to draw a joint picture of their fantasy land. Ask them to annotate their pictures with words for characters and objects.	
Communication: discussing their ideas collaboratively as a class	### Plenary Bring the children together to show their pictures and tell others about their imaginary land, perhaps making up a short story about what is happening there. Encourage discussion about their ideas. Keep work for future reference.	

DAY 5 ◢ Creating a magic castle

Key features	Stages	Additional opportunities

Creative thinking: generating imaginative ideas in response to visual stimuli and making connections through play

Introduction
Display the picture of a typical fairy tale castle from the CD-ROM. What would it be like to live there? Talk about a possible fantasy adventure set in this building. Who might the characters be?

Speaking and listening
Play some Elizabethan music and talk about how those who live in a castle might make their own entertainment. Compare the image of the castle from *The kiss that missed – extract 3* with the photograph of a real castle, both from the CD-ROM. Discuss similarities such as the turrets. Point to the dragon in the picture. Ask the children to think about why the dragon might be visiting the castle.

Independent work
Put the children into pairs to develop their ideas for a castle setting. Encourage them to use a range of methods to decide how their castle will look. In addition to drawing materials, provide small world equipment, blocks, collage, recycled materials and paint to model their ideas.

Communication: contributing individually to a class list

Plenary
Bring the class together to discuss their activities and how using the resources helped them to imagine their fairy tale castle setting. Invite the children to write a list of words about a fairy tale castle, beginning with words about their own castles. Save the list for future use. Invite suggestions for possible events that might occur in the castle.

Support: type with support to locate keys and spell words

Extend: use a keyboard to type words to describe their castles

Extend: read words from their own lists

DAY 6 ◢ Entering the world of aliens

Key features	Stages	Additional opportunities

Introduction
Ask the children to recall the story *Here come the aliens!* What did they like or dislike about it? Where was the story set? Who are the main characters?

Phonics: Inky pinky ponky, nicky nocky noo, KWAKK KWAKK

Social skills: listening to one another and respecting differences in ideas

Speaking and listening
Read the story again and display *Here come the aliens! – extract 2* from the CD-ROM, showing the spaceships heading for Earth. Compare this image with pictures of real spaceships. Are there any similarities? Who is inside the spaceships in the story? Look at pictures of the aliens. Do the children have a favourite? Which one is the ugliest? Read aloud some of their odd language.

Communication: working collaboratively in pairs to create their alien-carrying spaceship

Independent work
Put the children into pairs and supply them with card and brightly coloured pens. Invite one child from each pair to draw a picture of an alien and the other a spaceship. Explain that the alien must be small enough to fit into the spaceship. Encourage the pairs to discuss the shape and colour of the spaceship and alien before they start. Will they have any special gadgets? After the children have illustrated both sides of the spaceship they can cut it out. The finished aliens can then be cut out and glued onto the spaceship.

Plenary
Bring the class together and ask the pairs to talk about their work. Encourage positive discussion about similarities and differences. Hang the spaceships up with a caption 'Here come the aliens!' and invent stories about them.

DAY 7 ■ Predicting possible events on a fantasy walk

Key features	Stages	Additional opportunities

Introduction

Talk to the children about the fantasy worlds they have explored on screen and in pictures, books and the displayed extracts. Which did they like best?

Speaking and listening

Display *The kiss that missed – extract 2*. Would the children like to ride through those woods? Play some 'spooky' music and introduce words like deep, scary, dark and gloomy. Now show them *Here come the aliens! – extract 1*. Would the children like to walk on one of the planets pictured? Discuss how it might look, feel, sound and smell. Have the same discussion about the inside of one of the spaceships. Consider walking through other fantasy landscapes such as the giant's town or riding over the land of the witch on a broomstick.

Reasoning: considering possible events that might occur in their fantasy land

Independent work

Move into a hall or empty room, put the children into pairs and ask them to imagine that they are walking through a fantasy land together. Suggest that individual pairs choose the type of setting, for example, a deep dark wood, the bottom of the sea or a mystery planet. Ask them to talk to one another about possible events that might happen as they are walking along and re-enact them.

Creative thinking: generating imaginative ideas through role play

Plenary

Bring the class together and invite pairs to take turns to go on their imaginary walks, describing the landscape and re-enacting events. Discuss results.

Support: look at pictures and imagine walks in these settings

Extend: make dramatic interpretations of events and characters through role play and introduce appropriate dialogue

---

Guided reading

Ask questions to encourage children to predict possible events at different stages of the story.

Explain how the final phoneme in the words *kiss* and *miss* is represented by two identical letters and look for other examples of double letters in final phonemes, such as *ll, zz, ff.*

Assessment

Can children predict possible events in a narrative based on their experience of other texts during shared and guided reading?

Refer back to the learning outcomes on page 75.

Further work

Widen the range of evidence for predicting possible events in stories, for example, by reading books together, watching films, television programmes and theatre productions, and listening to CD versions of stories.

DAY 1 ■ Exploring characters' reactions to events

Key features	Stages	Additional opportunities
	Introduction Read *The kiss that missed* and talk about the knight. Explain that the children are going to explore what happens to him at different times during the story.	**Phonics:** up*o*n, k*i*ng, hu*rr*y, ki*ss*, h*o*t, b*a*d, ga*ll*oped, sme*ll*y **HFW:** once, Tuesday, was, good night, came, too, much, very, lived, here
Empathy: considering the thoughts, feelings and actions of the knight	**Speaking and listening** Display the first two pages and read the text together. Explain that the king's kiss starts the action. Explore the image of the knight mounting his horse. Discuss his clumsy attempts before finally galloping off. What does this show about his character? Display extract 2 from the CD-ROM of the knight entering the wood. How is he feeling? Ask the children to adopt a stance and expression to demonstrate this anxiety. Use photocopiable page 89 'Castle storyboard' to note the sequence of events in the knight's journey. Discuss how the kiss calms the wild creatures. Ask the children to adopt a stance showing the knight's pride when he returns the kiss to the king.	
Reasoning: predicting how characters will react in different situations	**Independent work** Put the children into groups to explore what happens to the wild creatures when they are kissed. Use a triangle to make a sound representing the light touch of the kiss and ask children to change from wild to mild when they hear it. **Plenary** Bring the class together to discuss how dramatising the movements of characters has helped them to predict how they will react in different situations.	

DAY 2 ■ Creating characters and setting for a story book

Tue

Key features	Stages	Additional opportunities
	Introduction Remind the children of the poses adopted for characters from *The kiss that missed*. Explain that, over the next few lessons, they are going to write a whole class adventure story and will begin by choosing characters and a setting.	
Communication: sharing their ideas for settings and characters in pairs	**Speaking and listening** Ask the children to recall fantasy stories and to describe some of the characters. Encourage them to think of good and bad characters, characters based on real people and fantasy characters. Explain that they will need to decide upon a suitable setting and a central character. Discuss a number of options for the setting of the story and choose the most popular.	**Support:** use photocopiable page 90 'Describe the moods' to collect ideas for poses
Empathy: considering the thoughts and feelings of their imaginary characters	**Independent work** Put the children into pairs to discuss their ideas for possible characters. Ask one child to adopt a pose in character to represent a reaction to an event, for example, showing happiness or anger, and ask the child's partner to guess the emotion. Suggest that the pairs take turns to use a digital camera to record their poses. Emphasise the need to take both whole body poses and close ups of facial expressions. Explain that the photographs will be used in their books. **Plenary** Bring the class together to demonstrate poses for the others to try to guess what prompted the emotion. Choose characters for the story and note them down.	**Extend:** develop awareness of how moods affect facial expressions by completing photocopiable page 90, writing down words associated with the facial expressions depicted

DAY 3 ■ Introducing a problem and resolution into a narrative

Wed

Key features	Stages	Additional opportunities
	### Introduction Ask the children to recall the events that happen in the story *The kiss that missed*. Explain that most stories follow a pattern with a problem to resolve. Can the children think of any problems in this story?	**Ext**~~end~~: complete ph~~otocopiable~~ page 91 ~~'Solve the~~ prob~~lem'~~
	### Speaking and listening Talk about the title of the story. What does it tell us about the main event? This is the first problem: the fact that the kiss missed. Because this happened then the knight was sent to catch it. Show the image of the knight encountering the next problem, getting through the dark scary wood with all the wild creatures. How is this solved? Continue to identify problem and resolution until the story ends. Explain that the main character in your class story will be involved in solving a problem. Remind the children of the chosen setting and characters by displaying this information for them all to see.	**Sup**~~port~~: read out wor~~ds~~ displayed on pape~~r or~~ a screen **Exte**~~nd~~: type their own ~~words to display~~
Social skills: developing collaborative writing by listening to and respecting other people's ideas		
Problem solving: identify problems and resolutions for a main character	### Independent work Put the children into the same pairs as Day 2 to discuss possible problems and resolutions. Supply them with their photographs from Day 1 to help with ideas. Ask them to re-enact them in order to decide upon the most effective. ### Plenary Bring the class together to decide upon an appropriate problem and resolution for the main character. Add this to the displayed notes and keep a copy.	

Day 2

DAY 4 ■ Retelling the whole class narrative

Thurs

Key features	Stages	Additional opportunities
	### Introduction Display the plan of the class story ideas from Days 1 to 3. Read through the notes together to remind children about their chosen setting, characters and conflicts and discuss how they arrived at their decisions.	
	### Speaking and listening Talk to the children about how their lists of settings and characters, their photographs and the written suggestions for problems and resolutions have helped them to create a possible adventure story. Take on the role of the main character and choose children to take on supporting roles. Decide together upon props to use and language to include. Use language related to the sequence of events such as *At first, next, then, in the end*. Afterwards, invite comments about your re-enactment and answer questions while still in role.	**Support:** offer support to help children get into role, both with language used and actions made
Evaluation: giving feedback and judging the effectiveness of their work	### Independent work Ask small groups of children to repeat the re-enactment while the others become the audience commenting on the production and suggesting ways of improving the action. Did the groups manage to organise the events into the correct sequence? Did they introduce appropriate story language?	
Communication: discussing their work collaboratively	### Plenary Bring the class together and have them decide whether they are satisfied with the adventure narrative they have composed. Which aspects are they particularly happy with? Which aspects do they feel they could improve upon?	

DAY 5 ■ Retelling own adventure narrative

Key features	Stages	Additional opportunities

Fn

Introduction
Remind the children of the process of creating a class narrative and explain that they are going work independently through the same process to compose and re-enact their own narratives.

Speaking and listening
Retell the class story to the children to refresh their memories. Provide them with their own drawings and photographs from previous lessons and suggest that they use them to create their own adventure story. Remind them of the need to have a problem for the main character to resolve.

Problem solving: identifying problems and resolutions for a main character

Independent work
Put the children into the same pairs as for Day 2 but ask them to work alone with their photographs and drawings until they are ready to retell or re-enact their story idea. Once they both have an idea involving a main character encountering a problem, encourage them to tell or act the story to their partners, showing the appropriate photographs and drawings. Encourage partners to ask questions and make suggestions about the way the story has been presented.

Support: children unsure of problem and resolution could complete photocopiable page 91 'Solve the problem'

Communication: discussing their work as a class and making constructive comments

Plenary
Bring the class together and invite children to take turns to use role play or storytelling to demonstrate their adventure narrative. Ask the others to make constructive comments about the presentation. Were they aware of the problem facing the main character and can they say how it was resolved?

Guided reading
Encourage children to identify problems and resolutions during guided reading. Draw attention to high frequency words in chosen stories and highlight them on given texts.

Assessment
Can children tell an adventure narrative during role play with events organised sequentially into problem and resolution during independent sessions?
Refer back to the learning outcomes on page 75.

Further work
Encourage children to identify problems arising in everyday situations and create a narrative involving one of these problems and an appropriate resolution.

DAY 1 ■ Walking through a fantasy setting

Key features	Stages	Additional opportunities
	Introduction Ask the children to recall the fantasy stories, films, photographs and pictures they have been exploring. Explain that, during the next few lessons, they are going to create an electronic book about a fantasy adventure together.	
Empathy: considering the thoughts, feelings and actions of their chosen character	**Speaking and listening** Begin by discussing the setting for the story. Display and discuss each of the following from the CD-ROM: the photograph of an under sea landscape; *The kiss that missed – extract 2* and *Here come the aliens! – extract 1*. Decide together in which of these settings they would like their adventure to take place and adopt this as the background. Choose a suitable main character. Will it be human, animal or alien? Invite the children to think about how this character would react if he/she took a walk through the setting.	
Creative thinking: generating imaginative ideas in response to visual and auditory stimuli	**Independent work** Put the children into pairs, display the chosen background and play an appropriate music clip to add atmosphere. Ask them to pretend to be the main character walking through the chosen setting and to comment on each other's actions. Invite them to think of words to describe their partner's mood.	**Support:** go into role in pairs **Extend:** introduce dialogue for a character during role play
Communication: communicating outcomes of discussion	**Plenary** Bring the children together to demonstrate their walks. Ask each pair to talk about the moods that they have portrayed, using their descriptive words. Encourage children to write these words on the display and save a copy.	

DAY 2 ■ Choosing a problem and resolution

Key features	Stages	Additional opportunities
	Introduction Remind the children that the planned outcome of this Phase is to write a short story, and talk briefly about the chosen setting and main character.	
Problem solving: identifying problems and resolutions for a main character	**Speaking and listening** Ask children to name stories they have explored and to identify the problem or problems the main character in the story had to resolve. Display the chosen setting background and write onto it the types of problems the main character might encounter in this environment, for example, getting lost, coping with wild or alien creatures or looking for a missing object.	
Evaluation: giving feedback to one another and judging the most appropriate option	**Independent work** Put the children into the same pairs and ask them to imagine that they are in the story setting. What problem might they have to overcome? Encourage them to re-enact their ideas and make notes before choosing one problem and a possible resolution to bring back to the whole class.	**Support:** help children to apply phonic knowledge to spell regular words **Extend:** type their ideas individually
	Plenary Bring the class together and ask each pair to talk about or re-enact their chosen problem and proposed resolution. Which problem would be the most likely for the setting and character, for example, encountering fierce sea creatures or managing to travel in space? Is the proposed resolution appropriate or can the children suggest a more suitable alternative? Write the final choice of problem and resolution on the displayed background and keep a copy.	

DAY 3 ◼ Planning out the story sequence

Key features	Stages	Additional opportunities
	## Introduction Remind the children of the problem chosen for the main character and the resolution. Explain that the next stage is to plan out the story in sequence.	
	## Speaking and listening Look through the stances on children's photographs saved from earlier sessions and refer to their mood lists. Would any of them link with the chosen problem, for example, holding up hands in the air in shock or being frightened? Choose images to represent the beginning, middle and end of the story and add them to the display. Explain that, once the story sections are written, the children can dress up and take further photographs of themselves in role to use in their finished book.	
Communication: working in pairs to decide upon an appropriate sequence for their story	## Independent work Put the children into pairs, and leave the image you have created on display. Supply each pair with photocopiable page 49 'My storyboard' and ask them to write a sentence about the beginning, middle and end of the story, using the images and mood lists to help them with descriptive and action words.	**Extend:** write story language independently to reflect the sequence of events
Evaluation: giving feedback and judge the most effective sequence for their story	## Plenary Bring the class together and invite them to read out their sentences. Use the sentence ideas and the action images displayed to decide upon an appropriate beginning, middle and end to the story. Type out a sentence for each section, modifying them until the children are satisfied and then keep a copy.	

DAY 4 ◼ Creating visual images for a storybook

Key features	Stages	Additional opportunities
	## Introduction Talk about how the children have decided upon the key features of their story, a setting, main character and problem to solve, and have established what happens at the beginning, middle and end.	
Social skills: listening to and respecting each other's ideas	## Speaking and listening Show the children a selection of images from a storybook with bold illustrations and a colourful background and contrast this with a storybook that is mainly text with few black and white drawings. Which do they prefer? Can they say why? How do they want their storybook to look?	
Creative thinking: generating imaginative ideas for the book images	## Independent work Put the children into small groups to discuss how they will create pages depicting the beginning, middle and end of their story. Explain that they will be able to add images, photographs or drawings to their chosen background using a computer or by hand. Let them discuss taking photographs of the main character. Which clothes and props will they need? Suggest that they draw each page, depicting where they will place the text and the image.	**Support:** draw pictures and write words about them **Extend:** plan out their pages complete with illustration and short sentence
Communication: discussing their ideas collaboratively	## Plenary Bring the class together and ask groups to feedback their ideas. Make notes and choose together the images to be created for four pages: opening page, problem presentation, resolution, conclusion, and how this will be done. Before the next lesson, ask a group to help take the photographs of a child in role.	

Tues

DAY 5 ■ Developing sentence structure

Key features	Stages	Additional opportunities
	Introduction Explain to the children that they are going to work on the sentences that will be added to the visual images they have created, to tell their story.	
Social skills: listening to others while they say their sentences and taking turns to say theirs	**Speaking and listening** Find a suitable poster or picture of some children carrying out an activity and ask the children to help you to write a sentence to say what is happening. Invite suggestions using the space available and write down exactly what each child says. What information does this sentence tell us? Talk about the sentences created. Which one is the most effective in conveying meaning? Draw attention to the structure of the sentence. Does it tell us anything about the characters and what they are doing? Ask individuals to point to the capital letter and full stop. Remind them that all sentences convey meaning, start with a capital letter and end with a full stop.	
Communication: working in pairs and discussing their ideas	**Independent work** Put the children into pairs and supply them with copies of photocopiable page 92 'Compose a sentence'. Ask each pair to look at the pictures of a story sequence and take turns to write a sentence underneath each one giving information about who is in the picture and what is happening to them.	**Support:** offer support with sentence structure and punctuation
Evaluation: judging the effectiveness of their writing	**Plenary** Bring the children together to read out their sentences and discuss the information they convey. Have they remembered correct punctuation?	**Extend:** take turns to type or write their sentences to display

DAY 6 ■ Writing sentences for an electronic book

Key features	Stages	Additional opportunities
Weds	**Introduction** Ask the children to recall features of sentence structure and punctuation and explain that they will be using this knowledge to write sentences for their book.	
	Speaking and listening Display the background screen chosen on Day 1 and then create four separate pages, for example, by printing or copying. Include one of the images of a child in role taken on Day 4 on each one. Experiment with adding clip-art or drawing objects that are vital to the plot. Ensure that the four pages reflect the opening page, problem introduction, problem resolution and story conclusion. Do the children feel their visual images tell the story in an exciting way? Continue to modify them until they are satisfied. Explain that they are now going to add some text to the four book pages.	**Support:** choose between clip-art options presented by the teacher **Extend:** show children how to explore clip-art independently or scan their drawings
Social skills: listening to and respecting other children's ideas when collaborating over their sentence writing	**Independent work** Put the children into pairs and display the opening page of the book. Ask them to work together to create an opening sentence to set the scene and introduce the main character. When the children are satisfied with their sentences, bring them together and ask them to compose a joint sentence. Modify it until all children are satisfied. Repeat the process with the remaining three pages.	**Extend:** design and use a paint program to create a title page
Communication: communicating outcomes orally	**Plenary** Read the four sentences in the finished book together. Discuss key aspects of the book making process and their successes and difficulties.	

DAY 7 ■ Planning individual stories

Key features	Stages	Additional opportunities

Thurs

Introduction
Print a copy of the children's book and read the paper and electronic versions to them. Explain that they are going to spend the next two lessons writing their own stories, choosing how they will go about it.

Speaking and listening
Ask the children to outline the process of writing a story from planning to completion. Tell them that they will be able to access all of the lists and notes they have saved from past lessons to help them with ideas. Ensure that they have ready access to copies of books featured in past lessons, art materials, puppets, dressing-up clothes, small-world characters and story bags. Explain that they will need to take turns to use ICT equipment such as computers, printers, scanners, digital cameras and recording equipment.

Social skills:
listening to each other's story ideas and making constructive comments

Independent work
Put the children into pairs and explain that they can spend the rest of the lesson discussing ideas for their stories and making notes ready to start the writing process in the next lesson. Encourage them to talk about how they might go about planning their story, for example, by getting into role or using small-world characters. Visit the pairs in turn to observe progress and make suggestions.

Support: get into role to explore story ideas, while an adult scribes for them

Communication:
discussing their plans together and modifying them if necessary

Plenary
Bring the class together to discuss their story plans. Suggest alternatives if any ideas are too complex or require resources that are unavailable.

Extend: take turns to read the story to each other

DAY 8 ■ Writing individual stories

Key features	Stages	Additional opportunities

Fri

Introduction
Ask the children to recall the individual story ideas they developed on Day 7 and explain that they are going to write down their stories and illustrate them.

Speaking and listening
Make a list with the children's help of the key features of narrative. Have they a suitable setting and main character? Is there a problem to solve? Can they think of a sentence to open the story and one to end it? Is there a catchphrase or repetitive language? Make sure that the children can read the words on the list and suggest that they follow it when they start to write their stories.

Support: with adult support, read the words on the list by applying their developing word recognition skills

Social skills:
listening to and respecting one another's ideas when developing sentence writing skills

Independent work
Put the children into pairs and supply them with photocopiable page 49 'My storyboard' to make notes and sufficient paper to try out different sentences. Encourage them to read their sentences to each other and decide whether they need modifying. Once they are satisfied that the sentences are correctly formed, and convey information about the beginning, middle and end of the story, suggest that they write each one on a separate sheet of paper, arrange the pages in order and illustrate them appropriately. If time allows, turn them into books with covers.

Extend: create electronic versions of their stories by typing them out and using paint programs or clip-art to illustrate pages

Evaluation: giving feedback to others and judging the effectiveness of their own writing

Plenary
Invite children to read their stories to one another and show the illustrations. Encourage positive comments and discussion about the key features of narrative they have included. Display the books in the book corner.

Guided writing

Encourage children to use ICT whenever possible to plan, record, write, illustrate, present and save their work.

Focus on appropriate use of language to ensure that events are organised sequentially into problem and resolution. During guided writing focus on the specific needs of the group, for example, reinforcing punctuation rules and ensuring that words are chosen to convey meaning.

Assessment

Can children compose sentences correctly demarcated by capital letters and full stops?

Can they write a story with the events organised sequentially into problem and resolution?

Ask children to complete the assessment activity, 'Writing a story' from the CD-ROM.

Refer back to the learning outcomes on page 75.

Further work

Challenge children to use a wider variety of ICT skills to illustrate their stories, for example, using digital photographs of objects or outdoor landscapes.

In the witch's cave

■ Look around the cave to find objects that the witch might use and draw a ring round them.

■ 100 LITERACY FRAMEWORK LESSONS YEAR 1

PHOTOCOPIABLE ■**SCHOLASTIC**
www.scholastic.co.uk

Illustrations © Andy Keylock / Beehive Illustration.

Name _____ Date _____

Castle storyboard

Once upon a time in this castle...

After that the...

In the end...

Describe the moods

■ Find words to describe the moods of the children on the sheet and write them in the boxes under the pictures.

■ 100 LITERACY FRAMEWORK LESSONS YEAR 1

PHOTOCOPIABLE ■SCHOLASTIC
www.scholastic.co.uk

Illustrations © Andy Keylock / Beehive Illustration.

Solve the problem

■ Read the problems in each box and write a resolution in the box underneath.

Problem Ben bear's mother went to look for some honey but Ben did not see her go. When he looked around she had gone.

Resolution

Problem Nazreen climbed up the tree, right to the top but then she got stuck and could not get down.

Resolution

Problem When the princess looked into the pond her crown fell off and sank right down to the bottom.

Resolution

Problem Little Red Riding Hood could see the wolf in the middle of the path but she did not want him to see her.

Resolution

Name _____   **Date** _____

Compose a sentence

■ Look at each picture and write a sentence about what is happening in the box below.

_____   _____

_____   _____

_____   _____

_____   _____

_____   _____

_____   _____

Illustrations © Andy Keylock / Beehive Illustration.

■ 100 LITERACY FRAMEWORK LESSONS YEAR 1

PHOTOCOPIABLE   **SCHOLASTIC**
www.scholastic.co.uk

NON-FICTION
UNIT 1 Labels, lists and captions

Speak and listen for a range of purposes on paper and on screen

Strand 1 Speaking
- Tell stories and describe incidents from their own experience in an audible voice.

Strand 2 Listening and responding
- Listen with sustained concentration, building new stores of words in different contexts.
- Listen to and follow instructions accurately, asking for help and clarification if necessary.

Strand 3 Group discussion and interaction
- Take turns to speak, listen to others' suggestions and talk about what they are going to do.
- Ask and answer questions, make relevant contributions, offer suggestions and take turns.

Read for a range of purposes on paper and screen

Strand 5 Word recognition: decoding (reading) and encoding (spelling)
- Recognise and use alternative ways of pronouncing the graphemes already taught.
- Recognise and use alternative ways of spelling the graphemes already taught.
- Identify the constituent parts of two-syllable and three-syllable words to support the application of phonic knowledge and skills.
- Recognise automatically an increasing number of familiar high frequency words.
- Apply phonic knowledge and skills as the prime approach to reading and spelling unfamiliar words that are not completely decodable.
- Read more challenging texts which can be decoded using their acquired phonic knowledge and skills, along with automatic recognition of high frequency words.
- Read and spell phonically decodable two-syllable and three-syllable words.

Strand 6 Word structure and spelling
- Spell new words using phonics as the prime approach.
- Segment sounds into their constituent phonemes in order to spell them correctly.
- Recognise and use alternative ways of spelling the graphemes already taught.
- Use knowledge of common inflections in spelling, such as plurals, -ly, -er.
- Read and spell phonically decodable two-syllable and three-syllable words.

Strand 7 Understanding and interpreting texts
- Identify the main events and characters in stories, and find specific information in simple texts.
- Explore the effect of patterns of language and repeated words and phrases.

Strand 8 Engaging with and responding to texts
- Distinguish fiction and non-fiction texts and the different purposes for reading them.

Write a wide range of purposes on paper and on screen

Strand 9 Creating and shaping texts
- Independently choose what to write about, plan and follow it through.

▶

UNIT 1 ◄ Labels, lists and captions *continued*

- Convey information and ideas in simple non-narrative forms.
- Create short simple texts on paper and on screen that combine words with images (and sounds).

Strand 10 Text structure and organisation
- Write chronological and non-chronological texts using simple structures.
- Group written sentences together in chunks of meaning or subject.

Strand 11 Sentence structure and punctuation
- Compose and write simple sentences independently to communicate meaning.
- Use capital letters and full stops when punctuating simple sentences.

Strand 12 Presentation
- Use the space bar and keyboard to type name and simple text.

Progression in information texts

In this year children are moving towards:
- Reading and using captions, labels and lists.
- Conveying information and ideas in simple non-narrative forms such as labels for drawings and diagrams, extended captions and simple lists for planning or reminding.

Key aspects of learning covered in this Unit

Enquiry
Children will ask questions arising from work on classroom routines and plan how to present the information effectively.

Reasoning
Children will explain why certain labels and captions are appropriate.

Evaluation
Children will discuss success criteria for their written work, give feedback to others and judge the effectiveness of their own work.

Social skills
When working with partners children will learn to listen and respond to others.

Communication
Children will develop their ability to discuss as they work collaboratively in pairs and in a whole-class context. They will communicate outcomes orally, in writing and through ICT if appropriate.

Prior learning

Before starting this Unit check that the children can:
- Tell you about the purpose of simple classroom labels and lists
- Read simple classroom labels with additional pictures or symbols
- Attempt to write labels, for instance in role-play area.
If they need further support refer to a prior Unit or to the Foundation Stage.

Resources

Phase 1: Objects for 'Favourite things' display; *Labels* by Fiona Tomlinson ✇; *Our favourite things* by Fiona Tomlinson ✇; Objects for a display linked to another area of the curriculum; Assessment activity 'Label the picture' ✇

Cross-curricular opportunities

Instruction texts and displays could be linked to other areas of the curriculum, for example toys

UNIT 1 ■ Teaching sequence

Phase	Children's objectives	Summary of activities	Learning outcomes
1	I know what a label is. I know what a list is. I can identify labels in the classroom. I can write labels and captions.	Make labels and lists. Write captions for a display. Identify the correct labels for objects. Independently write labels and captions	Children can say what the purposes of lists and labels in the classroom are. Children can give a complete sentence as a caption for an object or picture. Children can write a caption for an object or picture in a complete sentence with a capital letter and full stop.

Provide copies of the objectives for the children.

DAY 1 ■ Labels

Key features	Stages	Additional opportunities
	Introduction Prior to this Unit, ask the children to bring in and object such as a toy or book that they consider a 'favourite'. Make sure that they are able to leave it in the classroom for the week. Have a display area prepared for children to leave their objects. Ask some children to tell the rest of the class what their object is and why that object is their favourite.	**Phonics:** look at CVC words in the labels.
Enquiry: asking questions	**Speaking and listening** Discuss what the display should be called, for example, *Favourite things*. Tell the children that you want to write labels for the objects. Explain that a label says the name of the object. Ask the children for suggestions for each item. Focus on one-word labels. Write the chosen label on the card and display it next to the object. Make a list of the objects using the *Our favourite things* chart from the CD-ROM. List the objects as a book, toy, game, or other. Print out the chart when you have finished. Ask the children why they think we need to use lists. Suggest that they think about what they are going to do that day and then make a list to display.	**Extend:** write some of the list
	Independent work Invite the children to draw pictures to go with the list of what they are going to do that day. Display the list and some of the pictures.	
	Plenary Discuss why the children think lists are important.	

DAY 2 ■ Captions

Key features	Stages	Additional opportunities
Enquiry: asking questions	**Introduction** Look at the 'favourite things' display and read the labels. Ask the children if the one-word labels say enough about each object and if there could be more information. Tell the children you want to write captions for the objects. Explain that captions provide more information about an object. Model writing a caption for the first object. Make it a complete sentence and highlight the capital letter and full stop. Ask the children to count how many words you have written in the sentence.	**Phonics:** look at CVC words when reading and writing captions **HFW:** identify HFW when writing
Social skills: listening and responding; working collaboratively	**Speaking and listening** Put the children into pairs and ask them to think of captions for the other objects. Ask some of the children to say their captions and write them on the board. Deliberately leave out the capital letters and full stops and when you have finished. Ask the children if you have forgotten anything. Correct the sentences.	**Support:** some children will need more support to orally say their captions
	Paired work Ask the children why they think labels are important. Can they spot any other labels around the classroom?	**Sentence work:** identify full stops and capital letters
	Plenary Say that you are starting a new display based on a theme that you might be looking at in another curriculum area, for example, the seaside. Ask the children to bring in objects from home that will help make a display on this theme.	**Extend:** make a list of classroom labels

DAY 3 ▪ Writing captions

Key features	Stages	Additional opportunities
	Introduction Display *Labels* from the CD-ROM. Ask the children to identify whether the right label is with the right object. Cross out the label and write the correct label underneath.	**Phonics:** focus on CVC words in the labels
Social skills: working collaboratively	**Speaking and listening** In pairs, ask the children to think about a caption for one of the objects. Model writing some of their suggested captions and highlight the capital letter and full stop.	
	Independent work Invite the children to copy the caption from the board and/or try to write their own caption for one of the objects in the text on the CD-ROM.	**Extend:** find captions and labels in books
	Plenary Discuss with the children why captions are important. Where do they find captions in books or magazines?	

DAY 4 ▪ Writing labels

Key features	Stages	Additional opportunities
	Introduction Look at the objects the children have brought in from your request on Day 2 and some objects you have provided. Ask the children to talk about their object to a partner. Choose some children to stand up and talk about their objects to the class.	**Phonics:** encourage children to write CVC words independently using their phonic skills **HFW:** identify HFW when writing
Social skills: working collaboratively	**Speaking and listening** Ask the children to work in pairs and to tell each other what they think the label for their object would be. Then invite the children to swap the objects with another pair and think of a label for their new object.	
	Independent work In pairs, ask the children to write their own labels for the objects they now have. They should then write their labels on a piece of card.	**Support:** scribe for the children then let them copy the label onto a piece of card
Reasoning: explaining why certain labels are appropriate	**Plenary** Put the objects on a display and ask the children to match the objects to the labels they have written on the card. Ask the children if you have matched the correct label to each object.	

DAY 5 ■ Adding information

Key features	Stages	Additional opportunities
	Introduction Look at the display and the labels the children have made for the objects. Refer back to the 'favourite things' display and say that you think there should be more information. Model orally a caption for one of the objects.	**Phonics:** encourage children to write CVC words independently using their phonic skills
Social skills: working collaboratively **Reasoning:** explain why certain labels are appropriate	**Speaking and listening** In pairs, ask the children to make up a caption for their object. Ask them to repeat their caption to you and then ask if they think that their caption explains the object. Encourage them to make changes to their captions if necessary.	**HFW:** identify HFW when writing
	Independent work Invite the children to write their own captions for the objects on pieces of card. Remind them about capital letters and full stops.	**Extend:** write CVCC/ CCVC words independently
	Plenary Re-read the captions and put them beside the objects.	

Guided reading
Choose a non-fiction book and see if the children can spot the labels and captions. Ask the children what the book is about and what the captions and labels are showing.
See if the children can identify capital letters and full stops.

Assessment
Can the children explain the purpose of lists and labels?
Using the 'Label the pictures' interactive assessment activity on the CD-ROM ask the children to match the labels and captions with the pictures. Refer back to the learning outcomes on page 95.

Further work
Ask the children who need support to find labels and captions in other non-fiction books.
To extend the children provide opportunities for them to write lists in their structured playtime, for example, shopping lists in the home corner.

NON-FICTION
Unit 2 Instructions

Speak and listen for a range of purposes on paper and on screen

Strand 1 Speaking
- Tell stories and describe incidents from their own experience in an audible voice.

Strand 2 Listening and responding
- Listen with sustained concentration, building new stores of words.
- Listen to and follow instructions accurately, asking for help and clarification if necessary.

Strand 3 Group discussion and interaction
- Take turns to speak, listen to others' suggestions and talk about what they are going to do.
- Ask and answer questions, make relevant contributions, offer suggestions and take turns.

Read for a range of purposes on paper and on screen

Strand 5 Word recognition: decoding (reading) and encoding (spelling)
- Recognise and use alternative ways of pronouncing and spelling the graphemes already taught.
- Identify the constituent parts of two-syllable and three-syllable words to support the application of phonic knowledge and skills.
- Apply phonic knowledge and skills as the prime approach to reading and spelling unfamiliar words that are not completely decodable.
- Read more challenging texts that can be decoded using their acquired phonic knowledge and skills.
- Read and spell phonically decodable two-syllable and three-syllable words

Strand 6 Word structure and spelling
- Segment sounds into their constituent phonemes in order to spell them correctly.
- Recognise and use alternative ways of spelling the graphemes already taught.
- Use knowledge of common inflections in spelling, such as plurals, *-ly*, *-er*.

Strand 7 Understanding and interpreting texts
- Identify the main events and characters in stories, and find specific information in simple texts.
- Recognise the main elements that shape different texts.

Strand 8 Engaging with and responding to texts
- Distinguish fiction and non-fiction texts and the different purposes for reading them.

Write for a range of purposes on paper and on screen

Strand 9 Creating and shaping texts
- Independently choose what to write about, plan and follow it through.
- Convey information and ideas in simple non-narrative forms.
- Create short simple texts on paper and on screen that combine words with images (and sounds).

Strand 10 Text structure and organisation
- Group written sentences together in chunks of meaning or subject.

Strand 11 Sentence structure and punctuation
- Compose and write simple sentences independently to communicate meaning.

▶

UNIT 2 ◄ Instructions *continued*

■ Use capital letters and full stops when punctuating simple sentences.
Strand 12 Presentation
■ Use the space bar and keyboard to type their name and simple texts.

Progression in instructional texts

In this year children are moving towards:
■ Listening to and following a single more detailed instruction and a longer series of instructions.
■ Routinely reading and following written classroom labels carrying instructions.
■ Reading and following short series of instructions in shared context.
■ Contributing to class composition of instructions with teacher scribing.
■ Writing two consecutive instructions independently.

Key aspects of learning covered in this Unit

Enquiry
Children will ask questions arising from work on classroom routines and plan how to present the information effectively.
Reasoning
Children will make judgements on what is 'fact' and what is 'fiction' based on available evidence.
Evaluation
Children will discuss success criteria for their written work, give feedback to others and begin to judge the effectiveness of their own instructions.
Social skills
When developing collaborative writing children will learn about listening to and respecting other people's ideas.
Communication
Children will develop their ability to discuss as they work collaboratively in paired, group and whole-class contexts. They will communicate outcomes orally, in writing and through ICT if appropriate.

Prior learning

Before starting this Unit check that the children can:
■ Listen to and follow single instructions, then a series of two and three instructions.
■ Give oral instructions when playing.
■ Read and follow simple classroom instructions on labels with additional pictures or symbols.
■ Attempt to write instructions on labels, for example, in the role-play area.
If they need further support refer to a prior Unit or to the Foundation Stage.

Resources

Phase 1: Photocopiable page 108 'Sequence the game'
Phase 2: *How to play the beanbag and hoop game* by Fiona Tomlinson ✸; Photocopiable page 109 'How to write an instruction text'; Photocopiable page 110 'Sequence the beanbag game'
Phase 3: Instruction skeleton ✸; Photocopiable page 109 'How to write an instruction text'; Assessment activity 'Jam sandwich' ✸

Cross-curricular opportunities

PE

UNIT 2 ■ Teaching sequence

Phase	Children's objectives	Summary of activities	Learning outcomes
1	I can write simple labels independently.	Recall and act out the sequence of a PE game. Label photographs. Draw the sequence of a game	Children can listen to and follow simple instructions and write simple labels independently.
2	I can understand the difference between fiction and non-fiction. I can understand why we need instructions.	Sorting fiction and non-fiction texts. Discuss and highlight features of instructions. Understand the importance of instructions.	Children can say whether a text is a fiction or a non-fiction text.
3	I can write instructions.	Use an instruction skeleton frame. Create notes to help write instructions. Write instructions.	Children can write the next in a sequence of instructions, with the support of a partner. Children can write at least three instructions in a well-rehearsed sequence independently.

Provide copies of the objectives for the children.

DAY 1 ■ Discussing the sequence of a game

Key features	Stages	Additional opportunities
	Introduction This Phase is based on a simple game that you have created as a whole class in PE using a variety of small apparatus, for example, a throwing and catching game, jumping in hoops and so on. Ask the children to remember the game that they created in PE. (If it was the previous day they might need some help.) Discuss the sequence of the game and ask the children what they did first, next, after and so on, until the end of the game. Model the different 'steps' clearly.	
Social skills: listen to other people's ideas	**Speaking and listening** Ask the children to think about any games that they play in the playground. In groups of three or four, ask the children to play the games and explain the sequence to those who do not know how to play the game. You might want to go out into the playground to do this. You could also use small figures or objects for the children to use to 'act out' the game.	**Support:** suggest some games and remind children of how to play the game **Extend:** remember other games and put the instructions for how to play them into the correct sequence
	Independent work Encourage the children to draw a picture of a part of the game. Make sure they include the correct number of players and any apparatus.	
	Plenary Invite volunteers to demonstrate the game and explain the sequence.	

DAY 2 ■ Acting out a game

Key features	Stages	Additional opportunities
	Introduction Ask the children to sit in the same groups that they were in for the PE session in Day 1. Ask each group to come and demonstrate one stage in the game. Discuss with the rest of the class whether or not they have demonstrated the stage correctly. If not, ask a volunteer to come and explain the stage. When each group (or as many groups as it takes to finish the game) has demonstrated a stage and finished the sequence of the game, retell the game to the class and ask them if you have remembered correctly. Model appropriate use of language when they discuss the stages of the game such as words describing a sequence, for example *first*, *next*, *after*.	
Social skills: working collaboratively	**Independent work** In groups, ask the children to remember the game orally. Or give them figures and objects to 'act out' the game. If any disputes occur encourage the children to discuss their opinions with appropriate language.	**Support:** use the figures and objects with a group to 'act out' the game; stop at every stage and ask the children if they are remembering the game in the correct order
	Plenary Invite volunteers to use the figures to show you the sequence of the game. Play a simple game such as 'Simon says...'	

DAY 3 ▪ Labelling pictures

Key features	Stages	Additional opportunities
	Introduction In a PE session ask the children to play the game from Day 1. Use a digital camera to take pictures of the sequence. Ensure to get parents' or carers' permission before taking photographs. Download the pictures taken of the game onto the computer and display them so that the children can see them either on an enlarged print out or on a whiteboard. Discuss the pictures and what they can see in them.	**Phonics:** focus on CVC words and CVCC/CCVC words used as labels
Social skills: working collaboratively	**Speaking and listening** Invite the children to look at the pictures and discuss in pairs how they would label the different objects in the pictures. Ask a group to stand up and recreate one of the photographs of the game using any apparatus – as a freeze-frame exercise. Encourage one of the other children to write on a piece of card a label for one of the pieces of apparatus being used. Put the label next to the object.	**Support:** act as a scribe for the group and write the labels; ask one member of the group to put the labels next to the correct objects
	Plenary Give each group a copy of the pictures out of sequence and ask them to put the pictures in order showing the correct sequence of the game.	

DAY 4 ▪ Drawing a sequence

Key features	Stages	Additional opportunities
	Introduction Display the pictures of the game in the wrong order. Discuss the correct sequence with the children and put the photographs in the correct order. Using their knowledge from Day 3, ask the children to help you label the first picture.	**Phonics:** focus on CVC and CVCC/CCVC words
Evaluation: children begin to judge the effectiveness of their own instructions	**Independent work** Give each child a copy of photocopiable page 108 'Sequence the game' and ask them to draw the sequence of the game and write the labels. Ask them to discuss their choice of labels with a partner.	**Support:** scribe the labels for the children and encourage them to copy your writing
	Plenary Using the pictures as an aide-memoire, encourage the children to think about anything in the game that they would change. What have the children found the most difficult to remember or perform?	

Guided writing
Use the photographs to write a recount on what is happening in the PE game. Concentrate on full stops and capital letters.

Assessment
Have the children been able to label all the objects in the game?
Can they retell the correct sequence of the game?
Refer back to the learning outcomes on page 101.

Further work
For children who need support, reinforce the concept of sequencing using sequencing games, by sequence coloured beads and so on.
To extend the children, invite them to draw the sequence of the playground games from Day 1.

DAY 1 ■ Discussing Instructions

Key features	Stages	Additional opportunities
	Introduction Ask the children if they are happy with the PE game from Phase 1 and if there is anything they would like to change. Give the children some time to discuss before agreeing on some changes to the game. Suggest writing instructions so that other children can play it. Discuss the features needed for writing instructions such as: having a title, a list of what you need, what you do in the game and so on. Remind the children that instructions are written in sequence and are often written in numbered steps.	
Reasoning: make judgements on what is 'fact' and what is 'fiction'	**Speaking and listening** Show the children a variety of instruction texts and narrative texts. Using hoops or cards labelled *Fiction* and *Non-fiction*, ask the children to help you sort out what is a factual text and what is a fiction text. Look at the features of the texts.	**Support:** discuss each book with the children and highlight the differences
Social skills: working collaboratively	**Independent work** Put the children into small groups and give them a collection of narrative texts and instruction texts to look through. Challenge them to work together to put these into the two categories and talk together about their choices.	**Extend:** write a list of the features, with an adult acting as scribe if necessary
	Plenary Invite a child from each group to explain their reasons for the group's decisions.	

DAY 2 ■ Fact and fiction

Key features	Stages	Additional opportunities
	Introduction Ask the children in their groups from Day 1 to demonstrate one of the sequences of the game to another group. Then choose one of the groups to demonstrate to the rest of the class. Ask them to say orally what they are doing, for example, *I am throwing the ball to...* Write what the children say on the board. At the end of the game, re-read what you have written. Ask the children if the words sound like instructions or a recount/a story of what they have done. Change the *I* pronouns to *you* pronouns and ask the children if they think it reads more like a set of instructions.	**Phonics:** focus on CVC, CCVC/CVCC words when writing **HFW:** highlight any words such as: *and, the, at* and so on
Reasoning: make judgements on what is 'fact' and what is 'fiction'	**Speaking and listening** Display the text *How to play the beanbag and hoop game* from the CD-ROM. Talk about the differences between fact and fiction. Ask the children if the text is a story or instructions for something that someone can do.	
	Independent work Give each pair a copy of *How to play the bean bag and hoop game*. Ask them to highlight, with a pen or pencil, anything they think makes this text an instruction text.	
	Plenary Ask the children to show what they have done and explain their reasons.	

DAY 3 ■ Instructions around us

Key features	Stages	Additional opportunities
	Introduction Collect examples of instructions from around the school, such as, recipes, playtime rules and so on. Read them out to the class and ask the children if there is anything similar about the instructions, how they look, what words are used. Display the text *How to play the beanbag and hoop game* from the CD-ROM. Ask the children if the instructions they have just been reading and these instructions contain anything that is similar. Annotate the instructions with the similar features, for example, numbers. Display photocopiable page 109 'How to write an instruction text' and add any features to the list. Print out the list.	**Phonics:** focus on CVC, CCVC/CVCC words when writing **HFW:** highlight any words such as *and*, *the*, *at* and so on **Support:** enlarge a copy so the text is easier to read; work as the scribe for a group
Social skills: working collaboratively	**Independent work** Give the children a copy of another instruction text, for example, a recipe or playground rules. Working in pairs, ask the children to annotate it, highlighting any features that make it an instruction text.	**Extend:** write down an instruction and give it to a friend to see if they can follow it
	Plenary Ask the children to read and follow three instructions you give them, for example, *Tidy up the book shelves*, *Go and put your coat on your peg*, *Sit down on the carpet*.	

Guided reading
Read an instruction text. Highlight the capital letters and full stops. Count the words in the sentences – are they short sentences or long sentences? Ask the children if shorter sentences make the instructions easier to read. Focus on CVC, CCVC/CVCC and encourage the children to use their phonic skills to decode new words.

Assessment
Can the children sort a selection of books into fiction and non-fiction books?
Refer back to the learning outcomes on page 101.

Further work
For children who need support, reinforce features of instruction texts. Use photocopiable page 110 'Sequence the beanbag game' to sequence the pictures of the game in the correct order.
To extend children, encourage them to consider what would be important instructions and what are less important, for example, instructions on how to use a lifeboat on a ship and so on.

DAY 1 ■ Writing notes for a game

Key features	Stages	Additional opportunities
Social skills: listen to and respect other people's ideas	### Introduction Display the Instruction skeleton from the CD-ROM on the board. Explain to the children that this is a way of writing notes to remember the sequence of the game. Ask the children to recount the games. Make sure the children are recounting the sequence in the correct order. As they tell you the game, add notes to the skeleton frame. Show the print out of photocopiable page 109 'How to write an instruction text' and add any other features, for example, title, numbering. Print out the instruction skeleton. ### Independent work Ask the children to draw and write notes about a game on a copy of the instruction skeleton from the CD-ROM. ### Plenary Discuss with the children how to use their phonic knowledge to attempt to write new words. Write words on the whiteboard and demonstrate how to decode them, then say a word and demonstrate how to encode it and write it as you are spelling.	**Phonics:** focus on CVC, CCVC/CVCC words when writing **HFW:** highlight any words such as: *and, the, at* and so on **Support:** ask the group to draw the pictures and then act as a scribe on a 'joint' skeleton

DAY 2 ■ Using notes to write instructions

Key features	Stages	Additional opportunities
Social skills: collaborative writing; writing instructions	### Introduction Display the instruction skeleton on the board and add all the information from Day 1 by referring to the copy you printed. Tell the children that they are going to write up the instructions so that other classes in the school can play the game. Look at the first step. Model writing the title and ask the children what should be in the *You will need* box. Model writing the first instruction. Focus on the layout, full stops and capital letters. (Print out a copy of the instruction skeleton.) ### Independent work Invite children to work in pairs to write the next three instructions using the print out skeletons as reference. ### Plenary Review what the children have written, making any changes. Encourage the children to refer to the skeletons	**Phonics:** focus on CVC, CCVC/CVCC words when writing **HFW:** highlight any words such as: *and, the, at* and so on **Support:** encourage the children to write the next sentence independently focussing on CVC word spellings; as a group, write the next two sentences

DAY 3 Writing Instructions

Key features	Stages	Additional opportunities
	Introduction Review how to write instructions using photocopiable page 109 'How to write an instruction text' as a reference. Give the children the copies of the instruction skeleton you printed off on Day 2.	**Phonics:** focus on CVC, CCVC/CVCC words when writing. **HFW:** highlight any words such as: *and*, *the*, *at* and so on
Evaluation: giving feedback to others and judging the effectiveness of their own instructions	**Independent work** Independently, ask children to finish the instructions for the game. If the children have already finished, ask them to review their work with a partner and discuss what could be improved. Some children could write up their questions on the computer.	**Support:** as a group finishing writing the instructions; ask one child at a time to spell out CVC words
	Plenary As a class, make a display of the photographs and the written instructions. Ask the children how the display should look. If there is time, plan the display first on paper.	

Guided reading
Read an instruction text. Focus on CVC, CCVC/CVCC and encourage the children to use their phonic skills to decode new words.
Review the features of instruction texts, asking the children to highlight examples.

Assessment
Ask the children to complete the interactive assessment activity called 'Jam sandwich' from the CD-ROM. Refer back to the learning outcomes on page 101.

Further work
For children who need support provide them with other instructions, such as recipes, for them to reorder.
To extend children ask them to write their own basic recipe, for example for a fruit salad.

NON-FICTION ■ UNIT 2

Sequence the game

■ Draw the sequence of the game.

How to write an instruction text

A set of instructions needs:

- A title – what are the instructions for?

- A list – what do you need to complete the instructions?

- Pictures and/or diagrams.

- To be written in a sequence.

Instruction language

- Numbers and or words to show the sequence.

- 'Doing' verbs – the writer is telling the reader exactly what to do.

- Factual descriptive words – you do not use story words, for example blue crayon not the beautiful sea-blue crayon.

Add other features here:

Sequence the beanbag game

■ Cut out the pictures and put them in the correct order.

NON-FICTION ■ UNIT 2

Illustrations © Andy Keylock / Beehive Illustration.

NON-FICTION
UNIT 3 Recount, dictionary

Speak and listen for a range of purposes on paper and on screen

Strand 1 Speaking
■ Tell stories and describe incidents from their own experience in an audible voice.
Strand 2 Listening and responding
■ Listen with sustained concentration, building new stores of words.
Strand 3 Group discussion and interaction
■ Ask and answer questions, make relevant contributions, offer suggestions and take turns.

Read for a range of purposes on paper and on screen

Strand 5 Word recognition: decoding (reading) and encoding (spelling)
■ Recognise and use alternative ways of pronouncing and spelling the graphemes already taught.
■ Identify the constituent parts of two-syllable and three-syllable words to support application of phonic knowledge and skills.
■ Recognise automatically an increasing number of familiar high frequency words.
■ Apply phonic knowledge and skills as the prime approach to reading and spelling unfamiliar words that are not completely decodable.
■ Read more challenging texts which can be decoded using their acquired phonic knowledge and skills, along with automatic recognition of high frequency words.
■ Read and spell phonically decodable two-syllable and three-syllable words.
Strand 6 Word structure and spelling
■ Spell new words using phonics as the prime approach.
■ Segment sounds into their constituent phonemes in order to spell them correctly.
■ Recognise and use alternative ways of spelling the graphemes already taught.
■ Use knowledge of common inflections in spelling, such as plurals, *-ly, -er.*
Strand 7 Understanding and interpreting texts
■ Find specific information in simple texts.
■ Recognise the main elements that shape different texts.
Strand 8 Engaging with and responding to texts
■ Visualise and comment on events, characters and ideas, making imaginative links to their own experiences.

Write for a range of purposes on paper and on screen

Strand 9 Creating and shaping texts
■ Independently choose what to write about, plan and follow it through.
■ Convey information and ideas in simple non-narrative forms.
■ Create short simple texts on paper and on screen that combine words with images (and sounds).
Strand 10 Text structure and organisation
■ Write chronological and non-chronological texts using simple structures.
■ Group written sentences together in chunks of meaning or subject.
Strand 11 Sentence structure and punctuation
■ Compose and write simple sentences independently to communicate meaning.

▶

UNIT 3 ◄ Recount, dictionary *continued*

- Use capital letters and full stops when punctuating simple sentences.
Strand 12 Presentation
- Use the space bar and keyboard to type their name and simple texts.

Progression in recount

In this year children are moving towards:
- Describing incidents from own experience using sequencing words and phrases; listening to other's recounts and asking relevant questions.
- Reading personal recounts and beginning to recognise generic structure.
- Writing simple first person recounts linked to topics of interest/study or to personal experience, using the language of texts read as models for own writing, maintaining consistency in tense and person.

Key aspects of learning covered in this Unit

Enquiry
Children will ask questions arising from visits and/or events and activities in order to add greater detail.

Reasoning
Children will decide how to order recounts. They will learn to structure their speaking and writing into chronological order.

Evaluation
Children will discuss success criteria for their written work, give feedback to others and begin to judge the effectiveness of their own recounts.

Social skills
When developing collaborative writing, children will learn about listening to and respecting other people's ideas.

Communication
Children will develop their ability to discuss as they work collaboratively in paired, group and whole-class contexts. They will communicate outcomes orally, in writing and through ICT if appropriate.

Prior learning

Before starting this Unit check that the children can:
- Listen attentively to recounts and are able to recall some details including the correct ordering of events.
- Ask relevant questions and are confident to speak about their own experiences.
If they need further support please to a prior Unit or to the Foundation Stage.

Resources

Phase 1: Seaside holiday pictures ✇; Photocopiable page 120 'Features of a recount text'
Phase 2: *Oomph* by Colin McNaughton (Picture Lion); Moon, Desert island and Mountain photographs ✇; Recount skeleton ✇
Phase 3: *Dictionary* by Fiona Tomlinson ✇; Photocopiable page 121 'Alphabetical order'; *My school day* (core and differentiated) by Fiona Tomlinson ✇; Photocopiable page 122 'Sequence the day'; Assessment activity 'Using a dictionary' ✇

Cross-curricular opportunities

Geography – holidays, seaside

UNIT 3 ■ Teaching sequence

Phase	Children's objectives	Summary of activities	Learning outcomes
1	I can ask questions about a text.	Ask questions about holiday photographs. Sequence a picture recount.	Children can listen to a recount and ask questions to support their understanding.
2	I can identify the sequence of a recount. I know that a sentence has a full stop and a capital letter.	Use photographs as a stimulus for drawing pictures and writing notes for a recount.	Children can order events correctly. Children can identify and explain the main features of a sentence.
3	I can use a dictionary. I can write sentences using full stops and capital letters.	Explore how a dictionary works. Draw about a real event in school. Write sentences about an event in school.	Children can use knowledge of the alphabet to locate words in simple dictionaries. Children can write at least three simple sentences in the past tense and use some time connectives in a recount.

Provide copies of the objectives for the children.

DAY 1 ▪ Asking questions

Key features	Stages	Additional opportunities
Enquiry: asking questions	**Introduction** Ask questions such as: *Who has been to the seaside? What did you do there?* Display the first of the Seaside holiday picture sequence from the CD-ROM. Discuss with the children what they can see in the picture.	
Social skills: working collaboratively	**Speaking and listening** In pairs, ask the children to think of two questions about the picture, for example: *Who are the people?* Invite each pair to ask their questions in turn and provide the answers. (You might want to write down some of the answers to remind you, such as names.) If a question has already been asked, then it would be good to repeat the answer to remind the children.	**Support:** write out the following questions and give them to the children: *Who is in the picture? Where are the people? What are the people doing?*
	Plenary Write a question mark and a full stop on pieces of card. Ask one child to stand up and hold the pieces of card. Tell the class that the child with the pieces of card will hold one up. When they see a question mark they have to ask a question and when they see the full stop they have to tell you something. For example: *My name is...; The walls are painted blue. What is the name of your dog?* Ask the children holding the cards to get faster when showing them to the rest of the class.	

DAY 2 ▪ Practising a recount

Key features	Stages	Additional opportunities
	Introduction Display the first Seaside holiday picture from the CD-ROM again and then show the other pictures of the same holiday. Discuss what they children can see in the other pictures. Encourage the children to ask questions. Remind children of any names of people/places, and so on, from Day 1. Now demonstrate a recount using some of the information from the answers to the children's questions.	
Reasoning: ordering recounts **Social skills:** working collaboratively	**Speaking and listening** In pairs, ask the children to practise their own recount using a picture as a stimulus. Ask the partners to ask questions if they think any information might have been missed out.	**Support:** ask the children questions about the recount from the pictures
	Plenary Ask some pairs to tell their recounts to the rest of the class.	

DAY 3 ■ Discussing a recount

Key features	Stages	Additional opportunities
Reasoning: ordering recounts **Evaluation:** giving feedback about recounts	### Introduction Ask the children what makes a good recount. Remind them that a recount is not a story; it recounts an event or something that has happened to them in the past. List some words and ideas from their suggestions. Look at photocopiable page 120 'Features of a recount text' and read out the features. Add any extra features that the children think of when discussing recounts. ### Independent work Print out the Seaside holiday pictures from the CD-ROM. Separate the pictures by cutting each of them out. If possible, laminate them. Invite the children to sequence the pictures in the right order, and glue them onto another piece of paper if not laminated. ### Plenary Ask a child to help you write a sentence that you read to the class. Deliberately leave out the capital letter and full stop. If the class hasn't noticed the mistake, then ask them to tell you what is missing.	**Phonics:** focus on CVC, CCVC/CVCC words when writing **HFW:** highlight any words such as: *and, the, at* and so on

Guided reading
Read a story (a narrative) and then read a recount. Ask the children what they think the differences are between the two texts.
Encourage the children to decode CVC, CCVC/CVCC words using their phonic knowledge.

Assessment
Ask the children to listen to a recount and then ask if they have any questions.
Refer back to the learning outcomes on page 113.

Further work
Encourage the children who need support to ask questions about a story or recount by giving them prompt words such as: *who, what, when* and *where*.
Extend the children by asking them to draw their own holiday recount sequence. Give each drawing a title. They should swap with a partner and ask questions about each drawing.

DAY 1 ■ Drawing a recount

Key features	Stages	Additional opportunities
Enquiry: asking questions	**Introduction** Read a story about going on holiday such as *Oomph* by Colin McNaughton. Display the photographs from the CD-ROM of the moon, desert island and mountain. Ask the children questions such as: *Which place would you prefer to go to on holiday?* Say that they are going to pretend that they have been on holiday to one of the places in the photographs and that they should think about what it would be like there. Ask the children to give some examples.	**Phonics:** highlight in the text any CVC, CCVC/CVCC words **HFW:** highlight any words such as: *and, the, at* and so on
Reasoning: structuring a recount	**Independent work** Invite the children to draw pictures to go with a recount. Then ask them to practise sentences to go with their pictures orally, for example, *I went in a rocket and travelled to the moon.*	**Support:** write sentences with adult support **Extend:** write the sentences independently
Reasoning: ordering a recount	**Plenary** Let the children show their recounts to the rest of the class. Use some of the children's pictures to rehearse a recount with the whole class orally.	

DAY 2 ■ Making notes for a recount

Key features	Stages	Additional opportunities
Reasoning: structuring of a recount	**Introduction** Display the photographs of the moon, desert island and mountain from the CD-ROM. Remind the children what was discussed in Day 1. Display the Recount skeleton from the CD-ROM and use it to write notes about each of the pictures. (You may need to print out the pictures for reference when using the skeleton.) Explain that the skeleton frame is a way of writing notes to help remember word, phrases and events to write a recount. Notes can be one word or a phrase. You might need to print out the pictures and give a copy to pairs or groups of children.	**Phonics:** focus on CVC, CCVC/CVCC words when writing **HFW:** highlight any words such as: *and, the, at* and so on
	Independent work Print out the skeleton frame from the CD-ROM and give the children copies. Ask them to write their own notes about their holiday from Day 1. Cut and paste their drawings into the skeleton.	**Extend:** write two sentences for each of the pictures using their notes to guide them
Communication: communicating outcomes	**Plenary** Ask the children to think of two sentences for each picture and tell them to the child sitting next to them. Invite a volunteer to tell their sentences to the rest of the class. Discuss each of the illustrations. Encourage the children to ask questions.	

Guided reading
Read the book *Oomph* by Colin McNaughton or another book about a holiday and then ask the children to point out any difficult words. Ask the children how they try to read words that they have never read before. Encourage them to use their phonic skills.

Assessment
Write up some sentences of a fictitious holiday and muddle them up. Ask the children to put them in the right order.
Refer back to the learning outcomes on page 113.

Further work
Work with a group of children who need support to write a shared recount using the skeleton frame. Write notes and draw pictures.
To extend children, encourage them to use the skeleton frame on the CD-ROM to make notes about their own or a partner's recent holiday.

DAY 1 ■ Alphabetical order

Key features	Stages	Additional opportunities
	Introduction Display the *Dictionary* text from the CD-ROM. Highlight the features of the text: words listed in alphabetical order, any definitions of words, and so on. Ask the children if they can find some dictionaries in the classroom. Ask them if these dictionaries show the same type of information as the text on the CD-ROM.	**Phonics:** highlight in the text any CVC, CCVC/CVCC words **HFW:** highlight any words such as: *and, the, at*
Social skills: listening to and respecting other people's ideas; working collaboratively	**Speaking and listening** Before the lesson prepare some cards. Each card should contain a word that the children will be able to find in a dictionary. Tell the children they are going to play a game with a partner. Give one of each pair the cards. Ask the child to read out the word, their partner then has to find the word in the dictionary. Encourage the children to swap roles and repeat the process. They could time themselves to see how quickly they can find it.	
	Independent work Write some easy words on the board (ones that you know the class will be able to read and define). Write them randomly, not in alphabetical order. In groups, ask the children to put the words in order. They should discuss the correct order first, then choose a scribe to write them down alphabetically.	**Support:** give the children the alphabet as a reference and use photocopiable page 121 'Alphabetical order'
	Plenary Challenge the children to think of some definitions for the words. Write them on the board.	**Extend:** write their own definitions

DAY 2 ■ Drawing a recount sequence

Key features	Stages	Additional opportunities
	Introduction Display the text *My school day* from the CD-ROM. Read the text to the children. Ask them what type of writing this is, for example, is it a story or is it about a real place? Ask them what other features might help indicate what type of writing it is. Annotate the text using photocopiable page 120 'Alphabetical order' to prompt the children to look for the features of a recount text.	**Phonics:** continue to highlight in the text any CVC, CCVC/CVCC words bit also introduce any CCVCC/CCCVC words **HFW:** highlight any words such as and, the, at and so on
Social skills: developing collaborative writing **Communication:** developing ability to discuss	**Independent work** In pairs, ask the children to draw pictures for the recount, making sure that they have the correct sequence. After drawing, encourage each pair to tell their partner the sequence orally.	**Support:** in a group use the differentiated text
	Plenary Choose one pair of children to show their drawings to the rest of the class. Orally rehearse sentences for each picture to create a recount.	

DAY 3 ◼ Discussing an on-screen recount

Key features	Stages	Additional opportunities
Enquiry: asking questions	**Introduction** Find the 'At school' interactive poster from http://www.scholastic.co.uk/magazines/ and display it. Walk through the poster with the children. Discuss the photographs and the audio. Ask the children if there are there any differences between the children's own school and the school in the photographs on the interactive poster. Make a list on the board. Ask the children if they have any questions about the photographs.	
Reasoning: ordering recounts	**Independent work** Give each child a copy of photocopiable page 122 'Sequence the day' and ask them to draw their own day. Encourage the children to write notes or label their pictures.	**Extend:** write sentences instead of labels
Social skills: listening to others	**Plenary** Ask some children to read out their days. Highlight any differences that the children have noted and ask them why this is. Continue to reinforce the alphabet sequence and play an alphabet game such as putting the children in alphabetical name order when they line up to go out to play.	

DAY 4 ◼ Sequencing a recount

Key features	Stages	Additional opportunities
Reasoning: ordering recounts	**Introduction** Use a real event that has happened in the school, for example, a special assembly, or a trip out. Discuss what happened and make sure that the recount is in its correct sequence. Encourage the children to use appropriate language to describe the sequence such as: *next, then, after.* Use the recount skeleton frame to add notes.	**Phonics:** highlight any CCVC/CVCC words and continue to introduce any CCVCC/CCCVC words **HFW:** highlight any words such as: *and, the, at* and so on
Social skills: working collaboratively	**Independent work** Divide the class into groups. Ask each group to work on a particular stage of the recount. Tell the children to draw a picture to illustrate their stage of the recount. Ask the children to label their pictures.	**Support**: use photocopiable page 122 to help with the sequence of the event
	Plenary Select some children to show their pictures. Make sure that your selection shows the whole of the recount. Mix the children up and then ask if the rest of the class can put them back in order.	

DAY 5 ■ Making a class book

Key features	Stages	Additional opportunities
	### Introduction Before the lesson choose some of the children's drawings and any available photographs to scan into the computer. Explain to the children that you are going to make a class book or interactive poster using presentation software on the computer. Record some of the children reading the recount so that you can add them as audio files to the slideshow.	**Phonics:** highlight any CCVC/CVCC words in the notes and continue to introduce any CCVCC/CCCVC words **HFW:** highlight any words such as: *and, the, at* and so on
Reasoning: ordering recounts **Evaluation:** judging the effectiveness of the recount	### Independent work Ask the children to write sentences independently for each of the stages of the event using their drawings from Day 4 or photographs of the recount as a prompt. As a class create a slideshow file using the photos, some of the children's pictures and audio of the event you have been looking at. For each stage add the text the children have written. ### Plenary Show the slideshow recount to another class. Ask the children to review what they have done. Ask questions such as: *What was the hardest bit in the process?*	

Guided reading
Read children's own recount on the computer. Identify features of the recount. Ask the children to spell some of the words in the recount using their phonic knowledge.

Assessment
Complete the 'Using a dictionary' assessment activity from the CD-ROM. This activity should be done in small groups, one at a time, so that each child can use the same dictionary. Refer back to the learning outcomes on page 113.

Further work
Encourage children who need support to put the words on photocopiable page 121 into the right alphabetical order. To extend children, ask them to alphabetise some objects in the classroom, for example, the reading books or books in a book corner.

Features of a recount text

Recounts need:

■ To start by setting the scene – who, what, where, when, how?

■ To be written in chronological order – the events are sequenced.

Report language:

■ To be written in the past tense – it happened.

■ Time connectives – next, then after.

■ First or third person – I, me, you, we, or, he/she, they.

Add other features here:

Alphabetical order

■ Put these words in alphabetical order.

Grass	
Mum	
Open	
Play	
Stop	
Wish	
Xylophone	
Tip	
Box	
Frog	
Egg	
Help	

Jog	
Lump	
Not	
Dig	
Quick	
Rabbit	
Cat	
King	
Yes	
Zoo	
Violin	
Ant	
Into	

NON-FICTION ■ UNIT 3

Sequence the day

■ Draw pictures to show your school day. ■ Label the pictures.

NON-FICTION
UNIT 4 Information texts

Speak and listen for a range of purposes on paper and on screen

Strand 2 Listening and responding
- Listen with sustained concentration, building new stores of words.
- Listen to tapes or video and express views about how a story or information has been presented.

Strand 3 Group discussion and interaction
- Ask and answer questions, make relevant contributions, offer suggestions and take turns.

Read for a range of purposes on paper and on screen

Strand 5 Word recognition: decoding (reading) and encoding (spelling)
- Recognise and use alternative ways of pronouncing and spelling the graphemes already taught.
- Identify the constituent parts of two-syllable and three-syllable words to support the application of phonic knowledge and skills.
- Recognise automatically an increasing number of high frequency words.
- Apply phonic knowledge and skills as the prime approach to reading and spelling unfamiliar words that are not completely decodable.
- Read more challenging texts which can be decoded using their acquired phonic knowledge and skills, along with automatic recognition of high frequency words.

Strand 6 Word structure and spelling
- Spell new words using phonics as the prime approach.
- Segment sounds into their constituent phonemes in order to spell them.
- Recognise and use alternative ways of spelling the graphemes already taught.
- Use knowledge of common inflections in spelling, such as plurals, -ly, -er.
- Read and spell phonically decodable two-syllable and three-syllable words.

Strand 7 Understanding and interpreting texts
- Make predictions showing an understanding of ideas, events and characters.
- Recognise the main events that shape different texts.

Strand 8 Engaging with and responding to texts
- Select books for personal reading and give reasons for choices.

Write for a range of purposes on paper and on screen

Strand 9 Creating and shaping texts
- Independently choose what to write about, plan and follow it through.
- Convey information and ideas in simple non-narrative forms.
- Find and use new and interesting words and phrases.
- Create short simple texts on paper and on screen that combine words with images (and sounds).

Strand 10 Text structure and organisation
- Write chronological and non-chronological texts using simple structures.
- Group written sentences together in chunks of meaning or subject.

Strand 11 Sentence structure and punctuation
- Use capital letters and full stops when punctuating simple sentences.
- Compose and write simple sentences independently to communicate meaning.

Strand 12 Presentation
- Write most letters, correctly formed and orientated using a comfortable and efficient pencil grip.

▶

■ Write with spaces between words accurately.

Progression in information texts

In this year children are moving towards:
■ Conveying information and ideas in simple non-narrative forms.
■ Choosing what to write about, orally rehearse, plan and follow it through.

Key aspects of learning covered in this Unit

Enquiry
Children will ask questions arising from work in another area of the curriculum. They will ask relevant questions about why things happen and how they work, and explore how to find the answers using different sources of information.

Information processing
Children will use first-hand experience and simple information sources to answer questions. They will learn where to find information, understand what is relevant and use this to write their own pages for an information book.

Reasoning
Children will develop their concepts of fact and fiction and be able to explain why they have categorised a particular text.

Evaluation
Children will present information orally and in writing. They will discuss success criteria and judge the effectiveness of their own work.

Social skills
When developing collaborative writing, children will learn about listening to and respecting other people's ideas.

Communication
Children will develop their ability to discuss as they work collaboratively in paired, group and whole-class contexts. They will communicate outcomes orally, in writing and through ICT if appropriate.

Prior learning

Before starting this Unit check that the children can:
■ Understand that some books contain stories while others give information.
■ Read and write simple captions.
■ Join in with saying the alphabet.
If they need further support refer to a prior Unit or to the Foundation Stage.

Resources

Phase 1: Photographs of a hoop and stick and teddy bear ❦
Phase 2: _Teddy bears_ (core and differentiated) by Fiona Tomlinson ❦; Photocopiable page 140 'How to write a report'; _Toys long ago_ by Fiona Tomlinson ❦; _Video and computer games_ by Fiona Tomlinson ❦; Photocopiable page 141 'Teddy bear report'
Phase 3: Report skeleton ❦; Photocopiable page 140 'How to write a report'; Photocopiable page 142 'Report template'; Assessment activity 'Slinky' ❦
Phase 4: Photocopiable page 140 'How to write a report'
Phase 5: Report skeleton ❦; Photocopiable page 142 'Report template'

Cross-curricular opportunities

PE (hoop and stick)
History

UNIT 4 ■ Teaching sequence

Phase	Children's objectives	Summary of activities	Learning outcomes
1	I can ask simple questions. I can use information books, for example, indexes. I know the order of the alphabet.	Ask questions about a photograph. Look at how an information book works. Use an information books. Practical work on a topic. Practise alphabet sequence.	Children can ask simple questions. Children can identify a contents page and an index in an information text and they can use these to find the right page to answer simple questions
2	I know the difference between fact and fiction. I can identify the features of an information text.	Look at a variety of non-chronological reports and discuss the layout and language features. Compare information books and websites. Compare information books and fiction books. Turn an oral recount into sentences for an information book.	Children can say what the key structural features of a simple information text are. Children can say whether a sentence is in an appropriate style for an information text.
3	I can write a report text using appropriate sentences.	Use a report skeleton frame to write notes. Learn how to write a report text. Write a report text independently.	Children can write sentences for an information text in an appropriate style.
4	I know the difference between fact and fiction. I can identify the features of an information text.	Look at a variety of non-chronological reports and discuss the layout and language features.	Children can say what the key structural features of a simple information text are. Children can say whether a sentence is in an appropriate style for an information text.
5	I can write a report text using appropriate sentences.	Use a report skeleton frame to write notes. Children use the frame independently. Learn how to write a report text. Write a report text independently.	Children can write sentences for an information text in an appropriate style.

Provide copies of the objectives for the children.

Note about the Unit:
■ This Unit has five Phases however, Phases 4 and 5 are expected to be completed at another time of the school year, so that you can reinforce information texts using different themes or topics.
■ The work in Phases 3 and 5 could be repeated later using different content and extending demand. Ensure that children have appropriate specific phonic input during this time.

DAY 1 ■ Asking questions

Key features	Stages	Additional opportunities
TUES **Enquiry:** asking questions **Social skills:** working collaboratively	**Introduction** Display the photograph of the hoop and stick from the CD-ROM. Ask the children the question: *Can you see a hoop in the picture?* Then ask the children how they knew you were asking a question. Talk about the words you used, and the inflection of your voice. Ask more questions: *Do you think this is a toy? Is it a toy you might play with?* **Independent work** In pairs, ask the children to see if they can think of questions about the photograph. Prepare a list of oral questions. Let each pair ask the class their questions. Give time for the class to answer. Make a list of the questions and note down whether or not the children were able to answer them. Ask the children where they might find the answers to the questions they couldn't answer. Perhaps look for an answer to one of the questions. Discuss that some questions might not be able to be answered such as: *Who owns the hoop?* **Plenary** Look at contents pages and index pages and explain how they are used. Point out that they are both organised alphabetically.	**Support:** children will need help with what they might ask a question about

DAY 2 ■ Choosing books to find answers

Key features	Stages	Additional opportunities
Weds **Information processing:** locating parts of the books that give the information **Social skills:** working collaboratively	**Introduction** Before the lesson, choose a variety of information books. Make sure that you include some books on toys today and toys from the past as well as books on other subjects. Display the photograph of the hoop and stick and remind the children that this is a toy that was played with by children who lived in the past. Pose questions about what other toys children might have played with, for example: *Did they play with dolls?* Show the children the information books and ask them which book they think will help them to find that information. Observe whether the children can explain why they chose a particular book, for example, because of the cover photograph. Demonstrate using the contents and index page to find out information. **Independent work** Prepare questions based on the information books, for example: *How many wings does a butterfly have?* Divide the children into groups of three and give them a question. Ask them to find the book from your pile that might help them to find the answer. Taking turns, give the children time to look for their answer and then ask them to say what it is. Give them sticky notes to mark the useful pages. **Plenary** Invite the children to explain how they found the answer to their question.	**Support:** some children will need help using/reading the contents and indexes **Extend:** think of own questions to research

DAY 3 ◀ Finding information

Key features	Stages	Additional opportunities
Thur (handwritten) **Enquiry:** asking questions	**Introduction** Display the photograph of the teddy bear from the CD-ROM. Ask the children to think of questions to ask about the photograph. For example: *What is it? Who owns the teddy bear? Where does it live? What is it made of? Who made it?* Discuss what would be a good question and what would be a difficult question. There are questions that might not be able to be answered, such as: *How many teddy bears are there in the world?*	
Social skills: working collaboratively	**Independent work** Ask the children to work in groups and make up four questions about the photograph. Give another group their questions. In a specified time, for example 15 minutes, ask the children if they can find out the answer to the questions. Encourage the children to use the information books used on Day 2 and other books, as well as the internet. When the answers are found they can be told to the group that asked the questions.	**Support:** some children will need help writing and reading the questions
Communication: communicating outcomes	**Plenary** Discuss with the children if there were any questions they found hard to answer and any that they couldn't answer.	

DAY 4 ◀ Hoop and stick games

Key features	Stages	Additional opportunities
Fri (handwritten)	**Introduction** Display the photograph of the hoop and stick from the CD-ROM. Ask the children to think about questions relating to how the hoop and stick might been have used. Find out more information about hoops from the books used in Day 2 or from the internet.	
Social skills: working collaboratively	**Independent work** Take the children outside. (You might need extra adult helpers.) Hand out plastic hoops and sticks to pairs of children. Ask them to see if they can use the hoop in the ways that they have found out about. Challenge the children to measure the distance of how long they can keep the hoop moving before it falls down. Compare how they use the hoop up and down hill. Record the activity with a digital camera. Ensure to get parents' and carers' permission before taking photographs.	**Support:** some children will need help to keep the hoop moving and with measuring
	Plenary Ask questions about how well they did and what happened when the conditions changed, for example, when they took the hoop up and down hill.	

DAY 5 ■ Consolidating alphabetical order

Key features	Stages	Additional opportunities
Enquiry: asking questions **Information processing:** using information sources to answer questions **Social skills:** working collaboratively	**Introduction** Ask the children the question: *What other toys did children in the past use outside?* Use the books from Day 2 and/or the internet to find the answer to the question. Remind the children to use the contents page and the index to find information. Make a list of the toys that you find. See if you can find photographs of the toys and make a photograph display. **Independent work** Explain again how an index works alphabetically. Give groups of children words from an index of a book on pieces of cards and ask them to sort them alphabetically. Vary the number of words that you give to each group according to ability. **Plenary** Ask the children to say their alphabet. Ask if the children can arrange themselves in a line alphabetically by first name, and then by second name.	**Phonics:** highlight any CCVC/CVCC as well as any CVCC/CCCVC words **Support:** give some of the children the alphabet sequence

Guided reading

Read one of the information books that was used on Day 2. Read the book to the children and then let the children read it themselves. Discuss how they might attempt to read a word they don't know.

Assessment

Show the children an object – perhaps an old toy. Can they ask questions about it? Can the children use a contents and index page?
Refer back to the learning outcomes on page 125.

Further work

Some children may need further practice with alphabet sequence.
To extend children, ask them to find out how information pages on the internet work. (With hyperlinks and so on.)

DAY 1 ◢ Discussing information texts

Key features	Stages	Additional opportunities
Reasoning: developing concepts of fact and fiction	**Introduction** Show a teddy bear to the children and ask them to explain what it is. Can the children tell you any more information about it, other than its name? Say to the children that they are going to find out about teddy bears and display the text *Teddy bears* from the CD-ROM. Read the text to the children. Ask them if they think it is a story or is it about something that is real? Is it in a sequence like an instruction text? Does the order in which the information is written matter? For example, ask the children if they could they change around the paragraphs. Does the text has any pictures with labels and captions?	**Phonics:** highlight any CCVC/CVCC as well as any CVCC/CCCVC words in the text **HFW:** highlight any words such as: *and, the, at* and so on
Information processing: where to find information	**Speaking and listening** Using the books from Phase 1, Day 2, ask the children if they can spot layout features similar to the text. Use sticky notes to highlight similarities. Can the children identify any new features that they find? Ask the children to tell you the new features and add them to photocopiable page 140 'How to write a report' **Plenary** Look at the text *Teddy bears* and ask the children if they can see any capital letters and full stops. Is the text written in sentences?	**Support:** use the differentiated *Teddy bears* text from the CD-ROM; some children will need more support in identifying the features

DAY 2 ◢ Features of information texts

Key features	Stages	Additional opportunities
Information processing: how a report works	**Introduction** Display the text *Toys long ago* from the CD-ROM. Read the text to the children. Ask the following questions: ■ *Is it a story?* ■ *Is it in a sequence?* (It is not in a sequence like an instruction text but the paragraphs cannot be changed around because there is an introductory paragraph and the text is in an historical 'sequence'.) ■ *Does it have photographs with labels/captions?* ■ *Is it written in the first person, for example, does it say I or me?*	**Phonics:** highlight any CCVC/CVCC as well as any CVCC/CCCVC words in the text **HFW:** highlight any words such as: *and, the, at* and so on
Reasoning: developing concepts of fact and fiction	■ *Are there any characters in the text, for example, a princess?* ■ *Are there any story words that describe the characters, for example, a beautiful princess?* ■ *Are there any topic words, for example, names of toys?*	
Social skills: working collaboratively	**Independent work** In groups, invite the children to look at an information book and then a website. (All children should be monitored when looking at an internet page.) Ask them to compare the similarities and differences between the book and the website, for example: both have information text, the website has hyperlinks and so on. Ask the groups to present what they have found out to the rest of the group. **Plenary** Discuss with the children how labels and captions work. Can they tell you why they are used?	**Support:** work as a group and look at similarities first and then differences **Extend:** write notes about what they find out

DAY 3 ■ Highlighting special features of texts

Key features	Stages	Additional opportunities
Information processing: how a report works	**Introduction** Display the text *Video and computer games* from the CD-ROM. Read the text to the children. Look at the layout and the language of the text and highlight any features the children tell you. Refer to photocopiable page 140 'How to write a report'. If the children haven't spotted the *Did you know?* box, highlight this and ask if the children have ever seen this feature on another book.	**Phonics:** highlight any CCVC/CVCC as well as any CVCC/CCCVC words in the text **HFW:** highlight any words such as: *and, the, at* and so on **Support:** use the differentiated *Teddy bears* text from the CD-ROM; some children will need more support in identifying the features
Reasoning: developing concepts of fact and fiction	**Independent work** Working in pairs, give the children an information book and a fiction book. Ask them to discuss with their partner what the similarities and differences are between the two books. Use sticky notes to highlight any differences, such as: types of photographs and illustrations or text layout. **Plenary** If possible, show the children some old computer games and ask them to explain or give a report about the differences between the game and the games that they might play today.	

DAY 4 ■ Writing sentences for an information text

Key features	Stages	Additional opportunities
Information processing: how a report works	**Introduction** Before this lesson ask the children if they can bring in some old toys. Invite children in turn to come and talk about their toy, for example, what it is, where it comes from, how they got it, and so on. Choose one child and write what they say on the board, or record it on the computer and then write up what they have said. Discuss their oral text and ask the children if they would find this in an information book about toys. Ask the children if they can explain the differences, for example, that in an information book it is unlikely that they would see the pronoun *I*.	**Phonics:** highlight any CCVC/CVCC as well as any CVCC/CCCVC words in the text **HFW:** highlight any words such as: *and, the, at* and so on
Reasoning: developing concepts of fact and fiction	**Independent work** Give the children copies of photocopiable page 141 'Teddy bear report' and ask them to turn the sentences into an appropriate style for an information book. **Plenary** Display the text *Video and computer games* from the CD-ROM. Can the children identify any capital letters and full stops? Ask the children if all words beginning with capital letters are the start of sentences.	**Support:** teacher acts as a scribe **Extend:** write about their own toy and make a book

Guided reading

After reading an information book and identifying the features of the text, discuss the differences between fiction and non-fiction.

Assessment

Ask the children to orally change a sentence to sound like a report text. Sort books out into groups of non-fiction texts and fiction texts. Can the children tell you the key features of an information text?
Refer back to the learning outcomes on page 125.

Further work

Reinforce sentence work with children who need support.
To extend children, ask them to write a short report on the difference between old and new video/computer games.

DAY 1 ▪ Writing notes for an information text

Key features	Stages	Additional opportunities
	### Introduction Look at the photographs taken of the hoop and stick activity in Phase 1, Day 4. Discuss the photographs and ask the children to tell you what they did during the activity. Display the Report skeleton from the CD-ROM. Explain that this is a way of taking notes. Writing notes is a way of remembering information that they might write about. Explain also that the report skeleton will help them write as each of the circles on the skeleton means a separate piece of information. Demonstrate how to complete the report skeleton using the photographs and the children's memories to write notes about the hoop and stick activity. Print out the skeleton.	**Phonics:** highlight any CCVC/CVCC as well as any CVCC/CCCVC words
	### Independent work Display the photographs where the children can see them or make copies for them to share. Print out a clean copy of the report skeleton for each child and ask them to add their own notes and drawings to the skeleton using the photographs to aid their memory. Encourage the children to use their phonic knowledge when writing.	**Support:** some children will need help with writing the notes
	### Plenary View the skeleton and look at the photographs. Discuss if there is any more information that should be included. Ask the children to look at their own notes and add any information they have written. Keep a copy.	

DAY 2 ▪ Writing an information text

Key features	Stages	Additional opportunities
	### Introduction Display the report skeleton from the CD-ROM. Using the printed copy from Day 1, copy the notes on to the displayed skeleton. Explain to the children that you are now going to use the notes to write up the activity as an information text. Ask the children what the heading of the text should be and then write it on the board. Demonstrate writing the rest of the report using each circle in the skeleton as a new paragraph. Highlight any topic words and phrases and explain that these words might need further explanation.	**Phonics:** highlight any CCVC/CVCC as well as any CVCC/CCCVC words **Support:** create a group skeleton and act as a scribe **Extend:** write sentences to go with their pictures
	### Independent work Ask the children to draw pictures to go with the text and label or write a caption for them.	
	### Plenary Re-read the text about the hoop and stick activity to the children. Ask them to identify any features of the layout or language using photocopiable page 140 'How to write a report' as a reference.	

DAY 3 ◗ Writing notes for a report text

Key features	Stages	Additional opportunities
Information processing: learning where to find what is relevant and using it in their own writing	**Introduction** Ask the children to choose a toy from the past, for example a doll or a teddy bear, and explain that they will be writing notes using their own knowledge or information that they can find in books, on the internet. Tell the children to think about the following questions: *What is it? What is it made of? How old is it? When was it made? Who might have played with it?* **Independent work** Allow time for the children to do their research. Then, working in pairs, ask them to write up what they have found out about their chosen subject on a copy of the report skeleton. Encourage them to draw pictures to add to the skeleton. **Plenary** Reinforce how to write a sentence. Write some sentences up on the whiteboard without capital letters and full stops and ask the children to correct them.	**Support:** check the amount of notes/ information the children are including in their skeleton

DAY 4 ◗ Writing a report text 1

Key features	Stages	Additional opportunities
Information processing: understanding what is relevant	**Introduction** Before the lesson complete a report skeleton with notes from any toys in the past. Discuss the layout and language features of a report text: ■ Layout – heading, paragraphs, photographs with labels/captions ■ Language features – present tense, third person, no descriptive words, topic words Display the completed skeleton and quickly demonstrate how to write a heading and the first paragraph to the children.	
Evaluation: judging the effectiveness of their work	**Independent work** Using their skeletons from Day 3, ask the children to start writing their reports on photocopiable page 142 'Report template'. **Plenary** Ask the children to look at their skeletons and check if they have all the information they need to write their report in the template. Allow them to spend some time finding more information if they need to.	**Support:** some children might benefit from using a smaller template with less space to write in **Extend:** children could start to write their reports on the computer

DAY 5 ■ Writing a report text 2

Key features	Stages	Additional opportunities
	### Introduction Using photographs or drawings, demonstrate writing captions on the board. Highlight capital letters and full stops. Ask the children to look at their skeletons and see if they would like to add any other features, such as, a *Did you know?* box. Explain that *Did you know?* boxes usually contain interesting and unusual facts.	**Phonics:** highlight any CCVC/CVCC as well as any CVCC/CCCVC words
Information processing: writing pages of a report text	### Independent work Encourage children to continue writing their text using the skeleton notes they made in Day 3. When they have finished, ask them to draw pictures in their template and add labels or captions. Suggest that they add any other extra features they would like to.	
Evaluation: judging the effectiveness of their own work	### Plenary When children have finished writing their report, spend some time with them reading what they have written and their notes. Ask them if they have included everything from their notes.	

DAY 6 ■ Reading and reviewing the reports

Key features	Stages	Additional opportunities
Information processing: writing pages of a report text	### Introduction If some children still need more time to finish off their work from Day 5 then allow them this time. For any children who have finished writing their report, spend some time with them reading what they have written and their notes. Ask them if they have included everything from their notes.	**Phonics:** highlight any CCVC/CVCC as well as any CVCC/CCCVC words
	### Speaking and listening Ask some children to read out their reports to the rest of the class. If some children have written their texts on the computer, display them. Highlight any layout or language features.	**Support:** some children might prefer to have their reports read
Evaluation: judging the effectiveness of their own work	### Plenary Ask the children if they would change anything or add anything to their own reports. Make a display of the reports or create a class book.	

Guided reading

Look at the class writing from Day 2. Demonstrate how to evaluate the text and to make any appropriate changes.

Assessment

Monitor the children's work and if they are not using capital letters and full stops remind them to do so.

You could now use the assessment activity from the CD-ROM as the next two Phases are to be undertaken at a later stage of the year. Use the photograph of a slinky on the assessment page as a prompt for the children to write four sentences. Refer back to the learning outcomes on page 125.

Further work

Reinforce sentence work with children who need support.

To extend children, invite them to make the report texts into a class book.

DAY 1 ◼ Finding information

Key features	Stages	Additional opportunities
Information processing: locating parts of the books that give the information **Social skills:** working collaboratively **Communication:** communicating outcomes **Evaluation:** discuss success criteria	### Introduction Before the lesson choose a variety of information books on your chosen topic/subject. Display a photograph that shows something about the topic/subject you are covering. Ask questions about the photograph. Show the children the information books and ask them in which book they think they will find some information about the photograph. Can the children explain why they chose a particular book, for example, because of the cover photograph. Demonstrate how to find information you are looking for by using the contents and index page. ### Speaking and listening Prepare questions based on the information books. Divide the children into groups of three and give each group a question. In turn, ask them to find the book from your pile that might help them to find the answer. Give the children time to look for their answer and then ask them to say what it is. Provide children with sticky notes to mark the pages. ### Plenary Invite one child from each group to explain to the rest of the class how they found the answer.	**Support:** work with a group and read the question for the group; discuss which book would be appropriate before deciding which one to use **Extend:** write their own questions about a subject and give to another group to find out the answer

DAY 2 ◼ Reinforcing alphabetical order

Key features	Stages	Additional opportunities
	### Introduction Ask the children to recite the alphabet, using the letter names rather than the sounds. Display a large alphabet and ask the children to count the letters. Highlight the vowels. Highlight the consonants. Ask why it is important to know the alphabet. ### Independent work Spend a session playing a variety of alphabet games: ■ How many words can be made using each letter only once? ■ Alphabetise the children according to their first names/surnames. ■ Sort out words into the alphabet sequence according to the first letter. ■ Show the sequence of the alphabet, using cards showing each letter. Remove some of the letters and time the children to see how long they take to find out which are missing. ■ Draw in chalk on the playground the letters of the alphabet. Ask the children to find the first letter of their first name. Divide the children up into groups and ask each group to go to the first letter of the word you tell them. ■ Ask the children to tell you, for example, what letter is the third letter of the alphabet. Continue asking them which letter is which number in the alphabet. ### Plenary Ask the children when they think the alphabet is used in schools, (names in the register, in the library and so on).	**Support:** play matching games with each letter of the alphabet

DAY 3 ■ Layout features of a report text

Key features	Stages	Additional opportunities
Information processing: how a report works	**Introduction** Show an object (of your chosen topic/subject) to the children and ask them to explain what it is you are holding. Do they know more information about what it is, other than its name? Explain to the children that they are going to find out about the object and then read a text about it to the rest of the class. Can any of the children add any more information about the object?	**Phonics:** highlight any CCVC/CVCC as well as any CVCC/CCCVC words in the text
Social skills: working collaboratively	**Speaking and listening** Using the books from Phase 1, Day 2, ask the children if they can spot layout features similar to the text you have just read out. Use sticky notes to highlight similarities. Can the children identify any new features? Display photocopiable page 140 'How to write a report' and ask the children to help you to add any new features to it. Print it out.	**Support:** reinforce what the features of report texts are and highlight them in the texts **Extend:** write sentences for their objects
	Plenary Write a label or a caption for the object. Highlight the capital letter and full stop.	

DAY 4 ■ Language features of a report text

Key features	Stages	Additional opportunities
Reasoning: developing concepts of fact and fiction	**Introduction** Display a text about your chosen topic/subject. Read the text to the children. Look at the layout and the language of the text and highlight any features the children tell you. Refer to photocopiable page 140 'How to write a report'.	**Phonics:** highlight any CCVC/CVCC as well as any CVCC/CCCVC words in the text
	Independent work Working in pairs, give the children a non-fiction/information book and a fiction book. Ask them to discuss with their partner what the similarities and differences are between the two books. Use sticky notes to highlight any differences, such as: types of photographs and illustrations or text layout.	**Support:** if possible find some text to display on the whiteboard and use whiteboard tools to highlight the similarities and differences
	Plenary Ask a group to explain to the rest of the class what they have found out. Encourage the children to use appropriate language when describing non-fiction features.	

Guided reading
Read a report text and identify features. Look at the punctuation.

Assessment
Can the children identify features of a report text?
Refer back to the learning outcomes on page 125.

Further work
For children who need support, look at other examples of report texts and highlight the features.
To extend children, look at punctuation including, commas and question marks.

DAY 1 ◼ Using a report skeleton

Key features	Stages	Additional opportunities
Enquiry: asking relevant questions **Information processing:** understanding relevant information **Evaluation:** presenting information	### Introduction Display photographs of your chosen topic/subject. Discuss the photographs and encourage the children to ask questions. Display the Report skeleton from the CD-ROM. Explain that this is a way of taking notes, of remembering information that they might write about. Explain also that this will help them write as each of the circles on the skeleton means a separate piece of information. Demonstrate using the report skeleton, the photographs, any texts of your chosen topic/subject or other information that children already know about the topic. Print out the skeleton. ### Independent work Print out a clean copy of the report skeleton and ask the children to add their own notes and drawings using the photographs. Encourage the children to use their phonic knowledge when writing. ### Plenary Reinforce the features of a sentence. Write up some sentences on the whiteboard without capital letters and full stops. Ask the children to tell you where they would put a capital letter and full stop.	**Phonics:** highlight any CCVC/CVCC as well as any CVCC/CCCVC words **Support:** ask the children to draw each point 'fact' of the topic and then label the drawing

DAY 2 ◼ Using notes to write a class report

Key features	Stages	Additional opportunities
Information processing: learning how a report works **Evaluation:** communicating outcomes	### Introduction Display the Report skeleton from Day 1 on the whiteboard and add the notes from the printed copy. Add any more information from the children's own notes. Discuss the following: ■ Layout – heading, paragraphs, photographs with labels/captions ■ Language features – present tense, third person, no descriptive words, topic words. ### Speaking and listening Explain to the children you are now going to use the notes to write an information text. Ask the children what the heading of the text should be and then write it on the board. Demonstrate writing the rest of the report using each circle in the skeleton as a new paragraph. ### Independent work Divide the children into groups and ask them to draw pictures to go with a particular section of the text and label or write a caption for them. If there is time, scan in their pictures and use them to illustrate the text. ### Plenary Ask the children to look at their skeletons from Day 1 and see if they have all the information they need to write their report in the skeletons. Spend some time finding more information if they need to.	**Phonics:** highlight any CCVC/CVCC as well as any CVCC/CCCVC words **Extend:** highlight how they might use paragraphs to start a new point or 'fact' about the topic

DAY 3 ■ Writing individual report texts

Key features	Stages	Additional opportunities
	Introduction Tell the children that they are going to use their skeletons from Day 2 to write their own reports. Ask them to make a plan of the layout of their reports so that they know where any photographs or drawing might go. Discuss whether they could add other features such as a *Did you know?* box.	**Phonics:** highlight any CCVC/CVCC as well as any CVCC/CCCVC words
Information processing: writing pages of a report text	**Independent work** Ask the children to write up their texts using the skeleton notes they made on Day 1. When they have finished, they should draw pictures to go with their writing and add labels, captions and any other extra features, such as a *Did you know?* box.	**Support:** use photocopiable page 142 'Report template' **Extend:** encourage the use of paragraphs
Evaluation: judging the effectiveness of their own work	**Plenary** For any children who have finished writing their report spend some time with them reading what they have written and their notes. Ask them if they have included everything from their notes.	

DAY 4 ■ Reading and reviewing

Key features	Stages	Additional opportunities
Evaluation: judging the effectiveness of their own work	**Introduction** If some children still need more time to finish off their work, then allow them this time. For any children who have finished writing their report, spend some time with them reading what they have written and their notes. Ask them if they have included everything from their notes.	**Phonics:** highlight any CCVC/CVCC as well as any CVCC/CCCVC words
	Speaking and listening Ask some children to read out their reports to the rest of the class. If some children have written their texts on the computer, display them on the whiteboard. Highlight any layout or language features.	**Support:** some children might prefer to have their reports read
	Plenary Ask the children if they would change anything or add anything to their own reports.	

Guided reading

Use a current topic and ask the children to help you draw a skeleton that might help them make notes about the topic. Ask each child in the group to write up one of the points 'facts' from the skeleton. Support the children in spelling any CCVC/CVCC as well as any CVCC/CCCVC words using their phonic knowledge.

Assessment

Use the photograph on the assessment page as a prompt for the children to write four sentences in an appropriate style for a report text. Refer back to the learning outcomes on page 125.

Further work

With children who need support, reinforce the features of a sentence.

To extend children, encourage them to re-read their sentences and to make any corrections if necessary. Highlight any words or phrases that might not be appropriate.

How to write a report

A report needs:

■ To be non-chronological – it is not written in a sequence or like a story.

(Reports may include other text types like explanation or instruction.)

Report language

■ Present tense – it is happening now.

■ Third person – you do not use I and we.

■ General nouns – if you are writing about animals you call them by their animal name, for example cat not their pet name.

■ Factual descriptive words – you do not use story words, for example you would say the young princess not the beautiful youthful princess.

■ Topic words and phrases – these are special words that are used which relate to the topic you are writing about.

Other key features:

PHOTOCOPIABLE ■SCHOLASTIC
www.scholastic.co.uk

Teddy bear report

■ Turn these sentences into a report.

I love my toy he is soft and cuddly.

_____

I call him teddy bear.

_____

His arms and legs move.

_____

He was made in a factory.

_____

I bought him in a shop.

_____

Report template

■ Use this template to write your report. Write on the lines and draw pictures in the boxes.

NON-FICTION
UNIT 5 Recount (fact and fiction)

Speak and listen for a range of purposes on paper and on screen

Strand 1 Speaking
■ Tell stories and describe incidents from their own experience in an audible voice.

Strand 3 Group discussion and interaction
■ Explain their views to others in a small group, decide how to report the group's views to the class.

Read for a range of purposes on paper and on screen

Strand 5 Word recognition: decoding (reading) and encoding (spelling)
■ Recognise and use alternative ways of pronouncing the graphemes already taught.
■ Recognise and use alternative ways of spelling the graphemes already taught.
■ Identify the constituent parts of two-syllable and three-syllable words to support the application of phonic knowledge and skills.
■ Recognise automatically an increasing number of familiar high frequency words.
■ Apply phonic knowledge and skills as the prime approach to reading and spelling unfamiliar words that are not completely decodable.
■ Read more challenging texts which can be decoded using their acquired phonic knowledge and skills, along with automatic recognition of high frequency words.
■ Read and spell phonically decodable two-syllable and three-syllable words.

Strand 6 Word structure and spelling
■ Spell new words using phonics as the prime approach.
■ Segment sounds into their constituent phonemes in order to spell them correctly.
■ Recognise and use alternative ways of spelling the graphemes already taught.
■ Use knowledge of common inflections in spelling, such as plurals, -ly, -er.
■ Read and spell phonically decodable two-syllable and three-syllable words.

Strand 7 Understanding and interpreting texts
■ Identify the main events and characters in stories, and find specific information in simple texts.
■ Recognise the main elements that shape different texts.

Write for a range of purposes on paper and on screen

Strand 9 Creating and shaping texts
■ Convey information and ideas in simple non-narrative forms.
■ Create short simple texts on paper and on screen that combine words with images (and sounds).

Strand 10 Text structure and organisation
■ Write chronological and non-chronological texts using simple structures.

Strand 11 Sentence structure and punctuation
■ Compose and write simple sentences independently to communicate meaning.

Strand 12 Presentation
■ Use the space bar and keyboard to type their name and simple texts.

▶

UNIT 5 ◄ **Recount (fact and fiction)** *continued*

Progression in recount

In this year children are moving towards:
- Describing incidents from own experience in an audible voice using sequencing words and phrases such as 'then', 'after that'; listening to other's recounts and asking relevant questions.
- Reading personal recounts and beginning to recognise generic structure.
- Writing simple first person recounts linked to topics of interest/study or to personal experience, using the language of texts read as models for own writing, maintaining consistency in tense and person.

Key aspects of learning covered in this Unit

Reasoning
Children will sequence events using visual evidence.
Children will be explaining their opinions and returning to the text and their observations to find evidence.

Evaluation
Children will discuss success criteria for their written work and begin to judge the effectiveness of their own and others' writing.

Social skills
When developing collaborative writing, children will learn about assigning roles within a group to complete a task.

Communication
Children will develop their ability to discuss as they work collaboratively in pairs and groups. They will communicate outcomes orally, in writing and through ICT if appropriate.

Prior learning

Before starting this Unit check that the children can:
- Listen attentively to recounts and recall some details including the correct ordering of events
- Ask relevant questions and speak about their own experiences
- Discuss ideas confidently with a response partner.

If they need further support refer to a prior Unit or to the Foundation Stage

Resources

Phase 1: Photographs of a seed growing ✸; *Growing a seed* by Fiona Tomlinson ✸; Photocopiable page 153 'Sequence of how a seed grows'
Phase 2: Recount skeleton ✸; Photocopiable page 154 'Recount word band'; *Growing a seed* by Fiona Tomlinson ✸; Photocopiable page 120 'Features of a recount text'
Phase 3: Photocopiable page 122 'Sequence the day' (optional); Assessment activity 'An event' ✸

Cross-curricular opportunities

Science – growth of a seed
ICT – making an on screen multimodal text

UNIT 5 ■ Teaching sequence

Phase	Children's objectives	Summary of activities	Learning outcomes
1	I can sequence an event based on my observations.	Read a text and identify features of a recount layout and language. Put photographs in the correct order of events. Use a skeleton to sequence an event.	Children can sequence a set of events based on their own experience and observations.
2	I can tell a sequence of events using appropriate language. I can write about a sequence of events using appropriate language.	Model writing a recount. Orally finish a recount. Finish writing a recount in pairs.	Children can orally compose and retell a sequence of events using time connectives to link the sequence. Children can write a recount using time connectives to sequence events and correctly demarcate sentences.
3	I can use the computer to write a recount text.	Use software to present the recount using photographs and sound effects appropriately.	Children can write a recount using time connectives to sequence events and correctly demarcate sentences. Children can use software to present a recount using photographs and sound effects to create a multimodal text.

Provide copies of the objectives for the children.

DAY 1 ▪ Sequence words

Key features	Stages	Additional opportunities
	Introduction Prior to this Unit children will need to have had experience in growing seeds as part of a science project. Take photographs of the seeds at various stages of your project but, if this is not possible, there are photographs on the CD-ROM. Read and display the text *Growing a seed* from the CD-ROM. Ask the children what they can tell you about the text. Explain that it is describing a sequence, that it is describing the stages of growth of a seed. Ask them to find words that help show that it is a sequence: *first, then, next, after*. Highlight these words on the text.	**Phonics:** highlight any words which have long vowel phonemes in the text; ask the children to identify the letters that make the long vowel phoneme sound
Reasoning: sequencing events using visual evidence	**Independent work** Ask the children to draw the missing pictures from photocopiable page 153 'Sequence of how a seed grows' Encourage them to write about the stages under the pictures.	**Support:** write notes under the pictures **Extend:** write complete sentences
	Plenary Discuss what is similar about recount and story texts, that is, that they both can be in first person and in a sequence. Discuss what the differences are between recounts and story texts; recounts are always about real events.	

DAY 2 ▪ Correct order of a recount sequence

Key features	Stages	Additional opportunities
	Introduction Display the photographs of the seed growing either from the CD-ROM or from your own project. Make sure that they are not in sequence order and number the photographs (not in sequential order, but as you have displayed them). Discuss what is happening in each photograph and ask the children what they notice about the order they are in. Annotate the photographs, as the children make their observations. Give the photographs a new number relating to the order. Encourage the children to use words which describe a sequence: *first, then, next.*	
Communication: discussing as they work collaboratively **Reasoning:** sequencing events explaining opinions	**Independent work** If using your own photographs, print enough copies for the children to have one set between two. Ask the children to work in pairs to put the photographs in order. Suggest that they write notes to remind themselves which order they go in.	**Support:** discuss each photograph in detail before they decide on the correct sequence
Evaluation: discuss success criteria	**Plenary** Ask a pair to tell you their order and move your display set accordingly. Ask the class if they agree on this order. Make any changes if necessary.	

DAY 3 ▪ Writing recount notes

Key features	Stages	Additional opportunities
	### Introduction Display the Recount skeleton from the CD-ROM and explain what it is, that is, a way of making notes about a recount that helps to show the sequence of events. If possible, cut and paste the photographs into the skeleton. Ask the children to think of what happened at each stage when they were undertaking the science project of 'growing a seed'. Add some written notes to the skeleton. Print out the skeleton.	**Phonics:** highlight any words which have long vowel phonemes in the text; ask the children to identify the letters that make the long vowel phoneme sound
Reasoning: sequencing events	### Independent work Print out a clean recount skeleton. Ask the children to write up their own notes about what they did in the experiment, then to draw pictures.	**Support:** act as a scribe for the children to fill in a group skeleton
	### Plenary Print out the photographs of a seed growing from the CD-ROM or your own photographs and then stick them on the printed skeleton. Make a display of all the skeletons.	

Guided reading
Read a recount – a biography.
Ask the children to apply their phonic knowledge when reading.

Assessment
Ask the children to explain orally what they did the day before/in the morning. Check if they are following the correct sequence.
Refer back to the learning outcomes on page 145.

Further work
With children who need support, play sequence games to reinforce their understanding of sequencing.
To extend children, encourage them to use the skeleton to make notes of another event.

DAY 1 ◖ Using time connectives in recount

Key features	Stages	Additional opportunities
Reasoning: sequencing events **Social skills:** working collaboratively	**Introduction** Display the Recount skeleton and add in the detail that the children discussed in Phase 1, Day 3 and also the photographs, if possible. Explain to the children you are going to start writing the recount of the growth of a seed. Add the time connectives that the children identified in Phase 1, Day 1. Look at photocopiable page 154 'Recount word bank' and decide if there are any words on the list that they might be able to use. Orally model the first two steps in the recount sequence. **Independent work** In pairs, ask the children to finish off the next two steps of the recount orally. **Plenary** Ask the children to tell you what they have said. Ask if anyone has anything different. Are there any words that could have been used or detail that could be added? Add the time connective words to the skeleton and print it off.	**Support:** work as a group and help each other to say the next two steps of the recount orally

DAY 2 ◖ Features of a recount text

Key features	Stages	Additional opportunities
	Introduction Display the text *Growing a seed* and discuss and annotate the features of the text. Highlight the following features: ■ Heading ■ First paragraph tells us what the text is about – what is going to happen ■ The sequence ■ The past tense – words ending in *-ed* and *-d* ■ Time connectives. Use photocopiable page 120 'Features of a recount text' from Unit 3 and add any extra details the class finds. Then refer to the printed skeleton from Day 1. Model the beginning of the recount: the heading and the introductory paragraph. Then model the first two sequences in the recount.	**Phonics:** highlight any words that have long vowel phonemes in the text; ask the children to identify the letters that make the long vowel phoneme sound
	Independent work Using their skeletons and a copy of the class skeleton, ask the children to write more stages of the recount. Before they start, ask them to make a plan of the layout of their recount, as they will be able to either add their drawings from the skeleton to their writing or create new pictures.	**Support:** In a group act as a scribe for the children to finish the recount
Evaluation: discussing success criteria	**Plenary** Finish writing the class recounts, allowing the children to use their own recounts as a reference. Re-read the recount when you have finished.	

DAY 3 ■ Writing a recount

Key features	Stages	Additional opportunities
	Introduction Display the class recount from Day 2 and annotate the layout and language features. Refer to the skeleton to make sure that you have added all the detail. Ask the children if they would make any changes.	**Phonics:** highlight any words that have long vowel phonemes in the text; ask the children to identify the letters that make the long vowel phoneme sound
	Independent work Allow more time for the children to finish their own recounts. Add or draw pictures or if possible print out some photographs for the children to add to their writing.	
Evaluation: judging the effectiveness of their own writing	**Plenary** Read some of the class recounts. Ask the children to tell you whether they have added in all the detail from their skeletons and whether they would make any changes. Ask the children if there was anything they found hard when they were writing and anything they found easy.	**Support:** in a group continue to act as a scribe and then give time for children to add drawings

Guided writing

In advance, write a recount but miss out some key features. Ask the children to identify what is missing, and what can be added. Redraft the writing with the children.

Assessment

Ask the children to identify time connectives in their writing. Refer back to the learning outcomes on page 145.

Further work

With children who need support, use a recount text and highlight the time connectives. Ask each child to read the words, using their phonic knowledge. Discuss what the word means and why it is in the text.

To extend children, ask them to find out what the similarities and differences are between recount and instruction texts.

DAY 1 ■ Creating a presentation 1

Key features	Stages	Additional opportunities
	Introduction Explain to the children that they are going to make a presentation of the science experiment 'growth of seeds' and that they will need their recounts that were written in Phase 2. Demonstrate the presentation software and show them how to add text. Also show the children how to name and save their presentation.	**ICT:** using presentation software
Social skills: learning about assigning roles **Communication:** working collaboratively	**Speaking and listening** Divide the class into groups of approximately five and ask them to choose one of their recounts to type up into the presentation software. When they have chosen, ask them to choose who is going to type, or if they are going to share. Suggest that they might want to have someone reading out the recount, while someone else types the text. Next ask them to plan their recount. If needed use photocopiable page 122 'Sequence the day' from Unit 3 as a template for their plan. Ask the children to plan out what will go on every 'screen' or 'slide' of the presentation: text and pictures.	**Support:** most children will need help to type up their recounts; if it is possible, scan their recounts
	Plenary Ask the children to show their plans and ask them whether they have included everything from the recount. Ask them to identify whether they will be adding more pictures into the presentation than is on the recount. Identify which pictures they will want.	

DAY 2 ■ Creating a presentation 2

Key features	Stages	Additional opportunities
	Introduction Demonstrate again how to use the presentation software and then how to add photographs or scanned pictures into the presentation software.	**ICT:** using presentation software
Social skills: working collaboratively	**Independent work** Using their plans ask the children to begin their presentations. Tell the children that they have at least two days to do their presentations. (You may want extra adults to support the groups when they are using the presentation software.)	
Communication: communicating outcomes	**Plenary** Ask the children if they found the software hard or easy to use. Demonstrate again how to use aspects of the software that they found difficult.	

DAY 3 ■ Creating a presentation 3

Key features	Stages	Additional opportunities
	Introduction Review the layout and language features of a recount. Display a recount text and ask the children to highlight any features. Review how to use the presentation software and then how to add sound files to the presentation. (There are many places on the internet to find sound files you can download such as http://www.scholastic.co.uk/magazines/)	**ICT:** using presentation software
Social skills: working collaboratively	**Independent work** Let the children finish their recounts adding the text, pictures and any sound effects. Ask the children to look at other children's work and say one thing they like about it.	
	Plenary Display some text and ask the children to identify the sentences. Ask the children what makes a sentence. Ask them to check their presentation to make sure that they are using sentences.	

DAY 4 ■ Showing a presentation

Key features	Stages	Additional opportunities
	Introduction Remind the children of yesterday's work and explain that today they need to complete their presentations.	**Phonics:** check that the children are spelling the words with the correct long vowel phoneme
	Independent work Give the children more time to finish their presentations and then show them to the class. If possible, show the presentations to another class and ask this class for their responses to the presentations.	**Support:** use a template to write their review
Evaluation: judging the effectiveness of their own writing	**Plenary** Ask the children to write a review about making their presentations. Ask them to review what they found hard and/or easy. What did they like or not like about the presentation? What might they change? What might they add?	

Guided reading

In each group read their slideshow presentation (multimodal text) and identify the layout and language features of the recount. Ask the children if they can identify any punctuation. Then ask the children what is different about reading this on-screen text and the text *Growing a seed* they read in Phase 1.

Assessment

Use the assessment activity 'An event' from the CD-ROM and ask the children to write four sentences about an event or an observation of something in another lesson, making sure they use recount features such as time connectives. Ask children who need support to write three sentences or draw the sequence.

Refer back to the learning outcomes on page 154.

Further work

Play sequencing games to reinforce understanding.

To extend children, encourage them to create an animation sequence that can be added to the slideshow presentation.

Sequence of how a seed grows

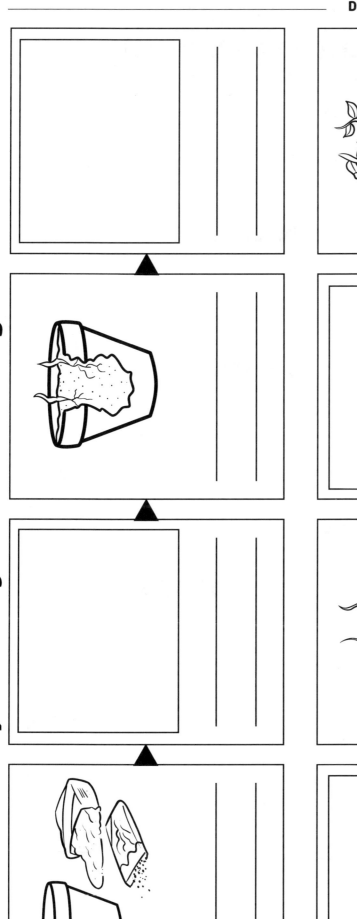

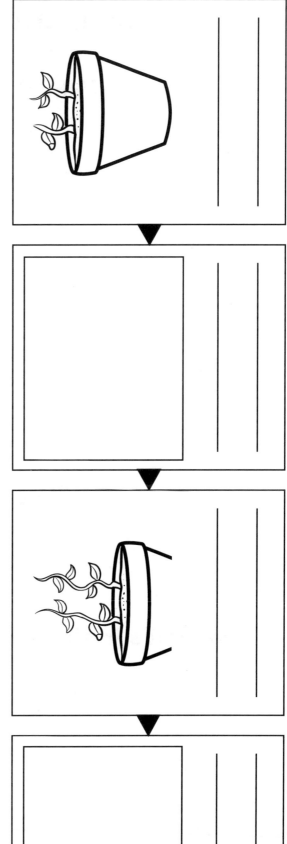

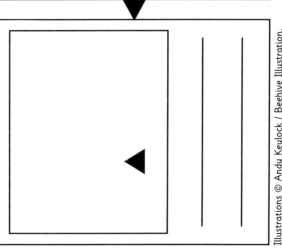

Illustrations © Andy Keylock / Beehive Illustration.

Recount word bank

What?

Then

After

Next

I

In 1900s

Finally

Later

You

He/she

-ed words in the past

Who?

Why?

When?

Were?

POETRY
UNIT 1 Using the senses

Speak and listen for a range of purposes on paper and on screen

Strand 1 Speaking
- Interpret a text by reading aloud with some variety in pace and emphasis.

Strand 2 Listening and responding
- Listen with sustained concentration, building new stores of words in different contexts.

Strand 3 Group discussion and interaction
- Ask and answer questions, make relevant contributions, offer suggestions and take turns.
- Explain their views to others in a small group, decide how to report the group's views to the class

Read for a range of purposes on paper and on screen

Strand 5 Word recognition: decoding (reading) and encoding (spelling)
- Recognise and use alternative ways of pronouncing and spelling the graphemes already taught.
- Recognise automatically an increasing number of familiar high frequency words.
- Apply phonic knowledge and skills as the prime approach to reading and spelling unfamiliar words that are not completely decodable.

Strand 6 Understanding and interpreting texts
- Spell new words using phonics as the prime approach.
- Segment sounds into their constituent phonemes in order to spell them correctly.

Strand 7 Engaging and responding to texts
- Explain the effect of patterns of language and repeated words and phrases.

Strand 8 Creating and shaping texts
- Visualise and comment on events, characters and ideas, making imaginative links to their own experiences.

Write for a range of purposes on paper and on screen

Strand 9 Text structure and organisation
- Find and use new and interesting words and phrases, including story language.
- Create short simple texts on paper and on screen that combine words with images (and sounds).

Strand 12 Presentation
- Write most letters, correctly formed and orientated, using a comfortable and efficient pencil grip.
- Write with spaces between words accurately.
- Use the space bar and keyboard to type their name and simple texts.

Progression in poetry

In this year, children are moving towards:
- Discussing own response and what the poem is about; talking about favourite words or parts of the poem; noticing the poem's pattern.
- Performing in unison, following the rhythm and keeping time.
- Inventing impossible ideas; observing details of first hand experiences using the senses and describing these.

UNIT 1 ◄ Using the senses *continued*

Key aspects of learning covered in this Unit

Enquiry
Children will play games and ask questions about what they can see, hear, feel (touch), smell and taste.

Reasoning
Children will explain the words they and others chose to describe objects and experiences.

Evaluation
Children will discuss success criteria for describing objects and experiences, give feedback to others and judge the effectiveness of their word choices.

Empathy and self-awareness
Children will hear or read about the sensory experience (and emotional reaction) of others and compare it to their own.

Communication
They will begin to develop their ability to discuss the language of poetry and to communicate their own observations and experiences through carefully chosen words. They will sometimes work collaboratively in pairs and groups. They will communicate outcomes orally, and in writing (possibly including ICT).

Prior learning

Before starting this Unit check that the children can:
■ Listen to poems being read and talk about likes and dislikes – including the words used.
■ Join in with class rhymes and poems.
■ Copy actions.
■ Enjoy making up funny sentences and playing with words.
■ Look carefully at experiences and choose words to describe.
■ Make word collections.
If they need further support refer to a prior Unit or to the Foundation Stage.

Resources

Phase 1: A bowl of soup; *Soup* by Barbara Moore ✇; Photocopiable page 166 'Soup'; Photocopiable page 167 'Foods'; *Tastes* by John Foster ✇; Photocopiable page 168 'Tastes'; *Sounds Good* by Judith Nicholls ✇

Phase 2: *Rosemary Rudd* by John Foster ✇; 'What is it like?' mind map image ✇; *Sniff, sniff, sniff* by Julia Donaldson ✇; Substances with strong smells such as ginger, coffee, lemon, bubble bath, toothpaste

Phase 3: West Midlands Safari and Leisure Park image ✇; Church, beach and classroom images ✇; *Noises off* by Gervase Phinn ✇

Phase 4: *I went to the farm* by John Foster ✇; 'What is it like?' mind map image ✇; Assessment activity 'Senses' ✇

Cross-curricular opportunities

Science (ourselves, sound and hearing, materials)
Art and Design (using materials)

UNIT 1 ■ Teaching sequence

Phase	Children's objectives	Summary of activities	Learning outcomes
1	I can listen to poems and identify words and phrases that describe what we can see, hear, feel (touch), smell and taste.	Discuss the five senses using soup as a stimulus. Read and discuss *Soup* by Barbara Moore. Recite the poem together. Complete a skeleton poem using a bank of words. Perform the poem. Read *Tastes* by John Foster. Analyse how it is built and rebuild the poem using word cards. Create a class poem. Create sound effects to accompany the poem *Sounds Good* by Judith Nicholls. Perform the poem.	Children can listen and respond to poems and identify words and phrases that describe what we see, hear, feel (touch), smell and taste. Children can recite poems in unison, following the rhythm and keeping time, inventing actions where appropriate.
2	I can identify details of sensory experiences and select descriptive words and phrases.	Discuss the experience of playing in the mud, using *Rosemary Rudd* by John Foster as a stimulus. Play in trays of different materials focusing on their feel. Complete a mind map of ideas about the feel of the materials. Read and discuss *Sniff, sniff, sniff* by Julia Donaldson. Play games to describe and identify smells.	Children can identify details of their sensory experience and start to select suitable words and phrases to describe these.
3	I can write suitable words and phrases to describe particular experiences.	Discuss image of a safari park and potential sensory experiences. Focus on one aspect and create own image and accompanying phrases for a display. Match images to verses in *Noises off* by Gervase Phinn. Create own phrases for the images, which address the other senses. Collate ideas as a class poem.	Children can identify details of their sensory responses to images and start to select suitable words and phrases to describe these.
4	I can write suitable words and phrases to describe particular experiences.	Choose six locations and describe what can be seen there. Using *I went to the farm* by John Foster as a model, work in groups to create verses to describe each of the six locations. Create a class poem from the group work. Present the poem using word processing and handwriting.	Children can identify detailed sensory responses to direct experience and start to select and write suitable words and phrases to describe these.

Provide copies of the objectives for the children.

DAY 1 ■ Soup – Barbara Moore

Key features	Stages	Additional opportunities
Communication: communicating observations and experiences	**Introduction** Use a bowl of warm soup to stimulate a discussion. Ask: *When is it eaten?* (For a starter; after a cold winter's walk; at a Bonfire party; when you've been ill.) *How does it make you feel? What flavour soups do you like? What does soup taste/look/smell/sound like when you eat it?* Explain that you are going to read and share a variety of poems that explore the five senses.	**Phonics:** *thick, thin, chin, gloop,* soup **HFW:** that, and, is, down, your, all
	Speaking and listening Display the poem *Soup* from the CD-ROM. Read it aloud with the children following. Invite them to join in. Ask: *How many times does the word soup appear?* (Highlight.) *Which two words describe what soup sounds like when it is being eaten?* (SLURP/GLOOP.) Can the children suggest sound effects for these words? *Which two words describe what soup feels like when it is stirred?* (Thick/thin.) Invite the children to identify the pairs of rhyming words. Suggest more words which rhyme with these. Discuss the meaning of *glorious*.	**Support:** stick the word cards onto the skeleton **Extend:** identify where capital letters are used
	Independent work Give each child photocopiable page 166 'Soup' with the missing words cut out and put in a bowl. Challenge children to match the words to the spaces to rebuild the poem.	
	Plenary Invite the children to bring their poems and bowls to the carpet. Hand out a spoon each to stir their imaginary soup in time with the rhythm of the poem as the whole class recites it with the agreed sound effects.	

DAY 2 ■ Tastes – John Foster

Key features	Stages	Additional opportunities
	Introduction Recap the experience of eating soup. Ask the children to suggest foods that are fun to eat and explain why. Use photocopiable page 167 'Foods' to give them some ideas, then add more. Record the children's suggestions and retain these for later use. Introduce the poem *Tastes*.	**Phonics:** cold, hold, sp*ice*, n*ice* **HFW:** is, and, to, of, are
Enquiry: asking questions about senses **Communication:** communicating observations and experiences	**Speaking and listening** Display *Tastes* from the CD-ROM and read it to the class. Can the children recall the six foods described in the poem? Hand out corresponding word cards from photocopiable page 167, as each is suggested. Read the poem again. Repeat for the adjectives used to describe each food. Using the food cards as prompts encourage the children to rebuild the poem, creating additional cards if required. Recite the poem as a class. Identify the two pairs of rhyming words *cold/hold, spice/mice*. Can they suggest other words which rhyme with cold and spice? Check understanding of new vocabulary. Discuss the value of the word *nice* as a describing word.	**Support:** assist children with segmenting sounds to enable them to spell them correctly; use photocopiable page 168 'Tastes' **Extend:** make a blank version of photocopiable page 168 'Tastes' for children to use
	Independent work Recap the fun foods suggested in the introduction. Let the children choose a food they love to eat and draw a picture of it and describe it.	
	Plenary Let children show and explain their work and piece suggestions together as a class poem. Recite the poem together. Compare with John Foster's poem.	

DAY 3 ▪ Sounds Good - Judith Nicholls

Key features	Stages	Additional opportunities

Introduction

Recap the work carried out so far, and then ask children to tell you sounds made when food is being prepared, cooked, served or eaten. Explain that today they are going to recite a poem about food sounds and make up sound effects to accompany the recital.

Phonics: crack/snap, fry/pie, grumbles/ rumbles
HFW: and, in

Speaking and listening

Display and read the poem *Sounds Good* from the CD-ROM with the children following. Ask them to identify rhyming words. Do they notice anything about most of the descriptions? (Use of alliteration.) Encourage children to identify the fact that the initial letters are the same. Why do they think the last line is in capital letters? (To be shouted!)

Alliteration: sausage sizzles and so on

Independent work

Split the class into three groups by ability. Allocate a verse to each group. Using percussion instruments and any other materials available around the class, (cups and straws, recyclable materials such as polystyrene trays and so on), ask the children to invent sound effects to accompany the words.

Extend: devise an additional verse, for example: Carrots crunch, Spaghetti slurps, Biscuits break and Babies burp!

Plenary

Evaluation: giving feedback to others

Perform the poem with sound effects - the whole class calling out *I'M HUNGRY* at the end. Ask each group to say what they liked about the other groups' work.

Guided reading

In a guided reading session, read all three poems and identify the pairs of rhyming words in each poem:
soup/gloop
thin/chin
cold/hold
spice/nice
fry/pie
grumbles/rumbles
Work together to find other words which rhyme with these pairs. Apply phonic skills to segment sounds into constituent phonemes in order to spell them correctly.

Assessment

At the start of each lesson, explain the objective of this Phase of work: to learn how to listen to, respond to and recite poems. Split the class into three assessment groups. Carry out summative assessment of one group on each of the three days of this Phase. Observing how the children work together and how they complete the task.
Refer back to the learning outcomes on page 157.

Further work

Using the school library and poetry anthologies available, make a collection of other food poems. Discuss the poems and encourage the children to explain which they like and dislike and to give reasons for these views. Invite children to bring in and share poems about food and the senses from home. Discuss which of the five senses each poem relates to. This work could be linked with the Design and Technology Unit – Eat More Fruit and Vegetables and a display made of the children's work. Make a recording of the recitals and place by the display.

DAY 1 ■ Rosemary Rudd - John Foster

Key features	Stages	Additional opportunities
Communication: communicating observations and experiences	### Introduction Ask if the children have ever played in mud. Discuss, compare and contrast experiences. Display and read *Rosemary Rudd* from the CD-ROM. Display and complete the mind map 'What is it like..?' from the CD-ROM using the phrases from the poem. ### Speaking and listening Display and read *Rosemary Rudd* again. Ask the children what the poem says mud is like, what you can do with it, and what it does. Complete the mind map using the children's responses and highlighting where each phrase appears. ### Independent work Put out trays containing different materials such as porridge oats, mud, sand, water, dough, clay. Place different objects/toys in each tray. Allocate a tray to each group of children and allow them a set time to explore the material in the tray. Ask them to focus on what it feels like, what you can do with it, and what it does. After the set time, move the children to a different tray and repeat. Ensure everyone experiences each material. ### Plenary Complete a mind map for each material experienced to describe the sensory experience and record their findings. Discuss the differences between the materials and highlight vocabulary which is particularly useful.	**Phonics**: Rudd, mud, toes, nose, hair, care **HFW:** I, like, it, is, you, can, up, and, gets, your, all, over, you, on, in, but, don't

DAY 2 ■ Sniff, sniff, sniff - Julia Donaldson

Key features	Stages	Additional opportunities
Communication: communicating observations and experiences	### Introduction Introduce a new smell or aroma into the room before the children come in, to stimulate a discussion. Lead into a discussion about favourite smells. Discuss smells experienced in different places (for example in the bathroom, kitchen, in a bakery, on a farm). Encourage descriptions of the smells suggested. ### Speaking and listening Display and read *Sniff, sniff, sniff* from the CD-ROM. Identify the repeated lines in each verse (first two and last). Highlight these. Once practised, invite the class to read the repeated lines with you filling in the description of the smell. Elicit what the three smells are (cheese, vegetables and socks) Ask: *How does the poem make you imagine the smells? Which words tell you that the smells are unpleasant?* ### Independent work You will need a variety of different substances with strong smells (ginger, coffee, lemon, bubble bath, toothpaste). Split the class into groups, each to be accompanied by an adult. Sit each group in a horseshoe with a volunteer sitting blindfolded in the opening. Offer them the smell to describe (encourage descriptions not guesses). Record useful vocabulary. ### Plenary Discuss the experience, likes and dislikes and what images the smells stimulated (family breakfast).	**Phonics:** sniff, **HFW:** what, can, you, a, of, all, in, that, I, can, the, have, been **Extend:** add adjectives to the smell once it has been described

Guided reading

Read *Rosemary Rudd* together and recap the vocabulary used to describe what mud does (*slips, slops, drips* and *drops*). Can the children think of any other words ending in *ps* to describe what mud does? (For example *plips, plops.*) Collect vocabulary to describe the experiences during the independent work. Work together to form a group poem based on the same structure as Rosemary Rudd – for example *Gary Grand says 'I like sand'.*

Assessment

While the children are working independently, make teacher observations both through questioning and without interaction. Record the vocabulary children use and their ability to select descriptive words and phrases which describe their sensory experiences.
Refer back to the learning outcomes on page 157.

Further work

Play other games to cover the other senses and make an interactive display of the games. For sound, use tape recordings of everyday events for the children to identify. For taste, identify different fruits when blindfolded (obtain parental permission first and check allergies). For sight, one child can hide from the class and describe an object to the rest of the class. The class has to identify what the object is. When correctly guessed, discuss which vocabulary was useful and other words which would help describe the object's appearance.

DAY 1 ▪ A visit to a safari park

Key features	Stages	Additional opportunities
Enquiry: asking questions about senses	**Introduction** Display the image of the West Midlands Safari and Leisure Park from the CD-ROM. Discuss a visit to an animal park and what the children may see, hear, smell, touch or taste there.	
Communication: communicating observations and experiences	**Speaking and listening** Model how to select suitable words to describe the features around the park, in terms of the senses they stimulate such as sweet-smelling hay, hungry bleating lambs. Annotate the image with the children's suggestions. Show them how to use a dictionary or word list to aid spelling and locate vocabulary.	
	Independent work Once the image has been annotated, put the children with response partners and allocate a specific area of the park to each pair. The pair should produce their own image of that area and come up with a simple descriptive phrase to describe a sensory experience for that particular area. Encourage the use of dictionaries or word lists.	**Support:** act as scribe then ask the children to copy your writing below **Extend:** write independently
Evaluation: giving feedback to others	**Plenary** Invite each pair to present their work to the rest of the class. Invite positive responses relating to the choice of words and encourage children to offer alternative vocabulary. Debate which are the most effective words. Display the children's images around the plan of the park. Word process descriptive phrases, enlarge and print off and display alongside the work.	

DAY 2 ▪ Noises off – Gervase Phinn

Key features	Stages	Additional opportunities
Communication: communicating observations and experiences	**Introduction** Display the photographs of a churchyard, a beach and a classroom from the CD-ROM. Encourage the children to suggest what they may hear in the different locations.	**Phonics:** -ing endings for verbs
	Speaking and listening Read Noises off from the CD-ROM to the class but omit the title for each verse. Can the children match the descriptions of the churchyard, beach and classroom to the images? Choose a different location such as a swimming pool or a zoo and create a class verse to extend the Noises off poem. Each line consists of a noun and a verb – encourage the children to retain this structure when creating their own descriptions.	
	Independent work Provide each child with a print out of one of the three images (mount on paper with a large border around for child annotations). Encourage discussion as to how the other senses would be stimulated and invite them to come up with phrases to describe what they may be able to see, feel, smell or taste if they were in that place, for example: people rushing. Assist with annotating the image with descriptive phrases. Encourage the class to be selective in their choice of vocabulary – using dictionaries or word lists where possible.	
	Plenary Combine the ideas into a new version of the poem entitled Senses off.	

Guided

Print out and cut up the poem *Noises off* into individual lines. Look at initial consonant clusters and encourage children to group together words which start with the same clusters. For example, *sl*ithering and *sl*iding; *sc*urrying, *sc*reeching, *sc*uttling, *sc*raping. Discuss what else makes each of these sounds.

Assessment

Mark each child's annotated image and provide feedback related to the suitability and quality of the words chosen, the application of phonic knowledge to spell the chosen words and the form and orientation of the letters.

Refer back to the learning outcomes on page 157.

Further work

Using images linked to work in history or other foundation subjects, ask the children to create phrases (noun and verb) to describe the sensory experiences which would be had in that image.

DAY 1 ◢ I went to the farm – John Foster

Key features	Stages	Additional opportunities
Enquiry: playing games about senses	**Introduction** Read the poem *I went to the farm* from the CD-ROM. Explain that you are going to create a class sensory poem based on *I went to the farm* but your poem is going to use a different location for each verse. Identify familiar places that the children have visited on days out, holidays, school trips and so on. Write suggestions on the board using the mind map images provided on the CD-ROM. Useful examples could be seaside, zoo, circus, fun fair, theme park, aquarium or museum. Decide on six locations.	**HFW:** I, went, to, the, and, what, did, see, a, at, me
Communication: communicating observations and experiences	**Speaking and listening** Make a list of all the different things that you may see at each of the locations. Add these to the mind map image from the CD-ROM. Encourage children to then describe their suggestion. If a clown is suggested, ask: *What is he like? What is he doing?* Continue questioning until the class agrees a suitable descriptive phrase such as a cheeky clown squirting water.	**Support:** work in a group with adult support
	Independent work Split the class into six groups – one location for each group. Invite them to decide on what they can see at that location and to draw a picture and accompany it with a descriptive phrase.	
	Plenary Come together and share the work carried out. Explain that the work is going to be saved to be used to create a class poem.	

DAY 2 ◢ Finding rhyming words

Key features	Stages	Additional opportunities
Communication: working collaboratively	**Introduction** Display the poem *I went to the farm* from the CD-ROM. Read the poem with the class following. What do they notice about the poem? There are six verses; the first line is repeated in every verse; the first line of each verse is a question and ends with a question mark; the first five verses have two lines which have a rhyming couplet – see/me and the last verse has three lines each of which rhymes see/me/tea.	**Phonics:** words that rhyme with *see* **HFW:** I, went, to, the, what, and, did, I, see, at, me, a
	Speaking and listening Ask the children to think of words which rhyme with *see* and record suggestions on the board. If the class has a rhyming dictionary demonstrate how to use this. Examples include: *chimpanzee, knee, tree, me, pea, sea, monkey, ski, happy, three.* Explain that they will now use the work from Day 1 to create their own verses.	
	Independent work Split the children into the groups they were in on Day 1. Invite each group to create verses for their allocated location. For example: *I went to the zoo and what did I see? A prowling lion which roared at me.*	
Evaluation: judging the effectiveness of word choices	**Plenary** Each group should recite their verses to the rest of the class. The class should then agree on the best verse from each group to be put forward to create the class poem.	

DAY 3 ■ I went to the zoo...

Key features	Stages	Additional opportunities
Evaluation: judging the effectiveness of word choices	**Introduction** Read the verses created on Day 2. Decide if any improvements or changes need to be made. Improve vocabulary if possible with more powerful verbs and adjectives. Decide in which order the verses are to be organised. Work together to create a third line for the last verse – revisiting the original poem to study the structure. Read the final version and ensure the class is happy with it.	**HFW:** I, went, to, the, what, did, I, see, a, and, at, me
	Independent work The class can now publish the poem using handwriting and word processing. Allocate children one verse each to write up and illustrate then assemble the six verses to produce a whole copy of the poem. While children are writing their verses, they can be invited to type a line each to produce a word-processed version of the poem. Demonstrate how to insert pictures or clip art to illustrate the poem.	**Extend:** write the whole poem and illustrate it
	Plenary Display the children's work and recite the class poem as a celebration of their work.	

Guided reading

Re-read all the poems used in Unit 1. Assess the different styles and structures of the poems. Look at rhyming patterns, high frequency words and so on. Discuss preferences and encourage children to explain these preferences.

Assessment

Ask the children to complete the assessment activity 'Senses' from the CD-ROM.
Refer back to the learning outcomes on page 157.

Further work

Create a sensory poem for an event being studied in History such as the Great Fire of London. This time have five verses and use a different sense for each verse. Model how to choose words and create useful rhyming couplets.

Soup

■ Put the poem back together again using the words in the bowl.

_____, _____, glorious _____,

_____ 'SLURP'

_____ 'GLOOP'

_____ thick,

_____ thin,

_____ dribbling

_____ chin!

✂ --

Soup	soup	soup	Soup	that	goes
And	soup	that	goes	Soup	is
And	soup	that	is	And	soup
that	goes	all	down	your	that

■ 100 LITERACY FRAMEWORK LESSONS YEAR 1

Foods

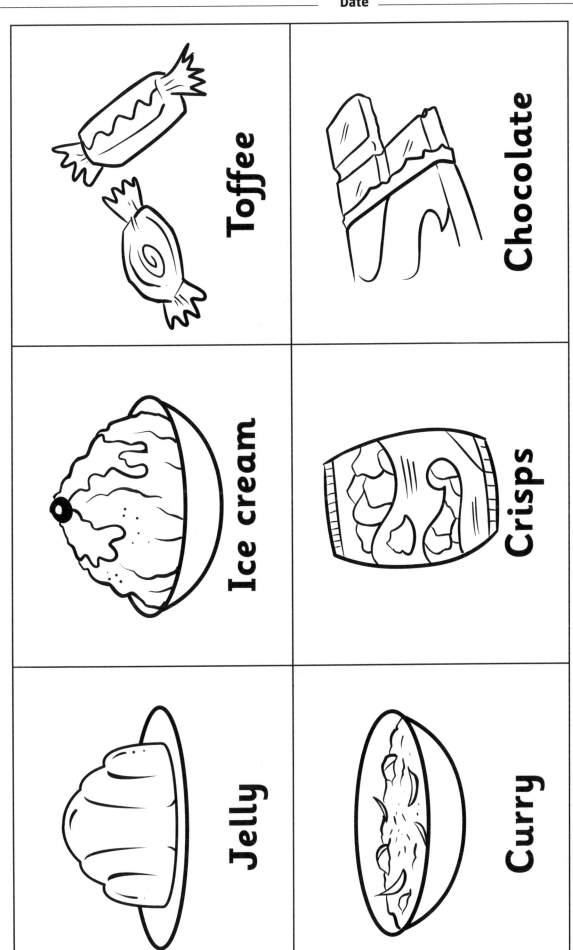

Toffee

Chocolate

Ice cream

Crisps

Jelly

Curry

Name _____ **Date** _____

Tastes

■ Add more words to the spidergrams.

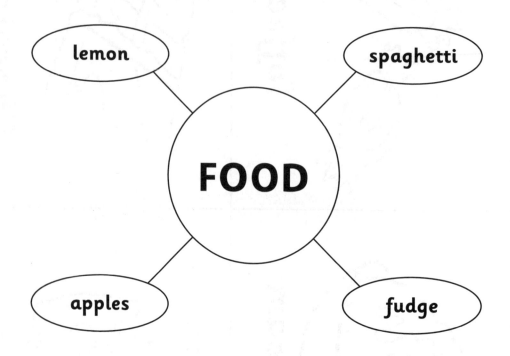

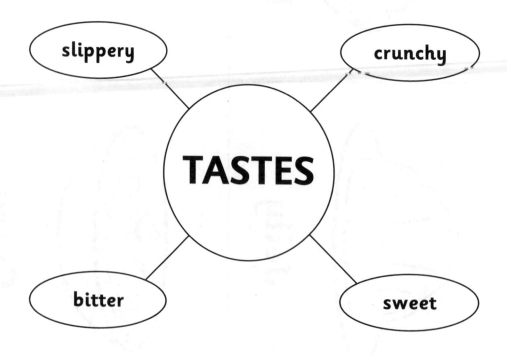

■ 100 LITERACY FRAMEWORK LESSONS YEAR 1

POETRY
UNIT 2 Pattern and rhyme

Speak and listen for a range of purposes on paper and on screen

Strand 1 Speaking
- Interpret a text by reading aloud with some variety in pace and emphasis.

Strand 2 Listening and responding
- Listen with sustained concentration, building new stores of words in different contexts.

Strand 3 Group discussion and interaction
- Ask and answer questions, make relevant contributions, offer suggestions and take turns.
- Explain their views to others in a small group, decide how to report the group's views to the class.

Read for a range of purposes on paper and on screen

Strand 5 Word recognition: decoding (reading) and encoding (spelling)
- Recognise and use alternative ways of pronouncing and spelling the graphemes already taught.
- Identify the constituent parts of two-syllable and three-syllable words to support the application of phonic knowledge and skills.
- Recognise automatically an increasing number of familiar high frequency words.
- Apply phonic knowledge and skills as the prime approach to reading and spelling unfamiliar words that are not completely decodable.
- Read more challenging texts which can be decoded using their acquired phonic knowledge and skills, along with automatic recognition of high frequency words.
- Read and spell phonically decodable two-syllable and three-syllable words.

Strand 6 Understanding and interpreting texts
- Spell new words using phonics as the prime approach.
- Segment sounds into their constituent phonemes in order to spell them correctly.
- Recognise and use alternative ways of spelling the graphemes already taught.
- Use knowledge of common inflections in spelling, such as plurals, *-ly, -er*.
- Read and spell phonically decodable two-syllable and three-syllable words.

Strand 7 Engaging and responding to texts
- Explain the effect of patterns of language and repeated words and phrases.

Strand 8 Creating and shaping texts
- Visualise and comment on events, characters and ideas, making imaginative links to their own experiences.

Write for a range of purposes on paper and on screen

Strand 9 Text structure and organisation
- Find and use new and interesting words and phrases, including story language.
- Create short simple texts on paper and on screen that combine words with images (and sounds).

Strand 12 Presentation
- Write most letters, correctly formed and orientated, using a comfortable and efficient pencil grip.
- Write with spaces between words accurately.

UNIT 2 ◀ Pattern and rhyme *continued*

Progression in poetry

In this year, children are moving towards:
- Noticing the poem's pattern.
- Performing in unison, following the rhythm and keeping time.
- Imitating and inventing actions.
- Inventing impossible ideas.
- Listing words and phrases or using a repeating pattern or line.

Key aspects of learning covered in this Unit

Enquiry
Children will hear, read and respond to rhymes and simple patterned stories, exploring the patterns created by words and phrases.
Reasoning
Children will explain the words they and others chose to complete their compositions.
Evaluation
Children will record their composition on audio or video as a vehicle for review.
Empathy and Self-awareness
Children will hear the patterns created by others and discuss their views – giving positive and constructive feedback.
Communication
They will begin to develop their ability to discuss the language of poetry and to communicate through carefully chosen words. They will sometimes work collaboratively in pairs or in groups and will communicate outcomes orally and in writing (possibly using ICT).

Prior learning

Before starting this Unit check that the children can:
- Listen to poems being read and talk about likes and dislikes – including the words used.
- Join in with class rhymes.
- Copy actions.
- Enjoy making up funny sentences and playing with words.
- Make word collections.
If they need further support refer to a prior Unit or to the Foundation Stage.

Resources

Phase 1: *The pirate ship song* ❧; Photocopiable page 179 'Number rhymes'; Photocopiable page 180 'The pirate ship song'
Phase 2: *Playdough people* by Tony Mitton ❧; Play dough
Phase 3: *The Smartest Giant in Town* by Julia Donaldson
Phase 4: *Daisy Artichoke* by Quentin Blake ❧; *Fantastic Daisy Artichoke* by Quentin Blake; *Betty Bittersweet* by Sylvia Clements ❧; Interactive activity 'Betty Bittersweet' ❧; Assessment activity 'Phonics sorting game' ❧

Cross-curricular opportunities

Science (ourselves)
Art and design

UNIT 2 ■ Teaching sequence

Phase	Children's objectives	Summary of activities	Learning outcomes
1	I can recite simple rhymes with predictable and repeating patterns. I can substitute and extend the patterns in rhymes and verses through language play.	Learn the words and actions to *The pirate ship song*. List rhyming words for the numbers one to ten. Make up rhyming couplets for the numbers 1 to ten. Agree a class version of the song. Write up the class poem on the pirate ship templates provided. Record the recital of the performance either on audio or video.	Children can recite rhymes with repeating and predictable patterns using actions. Children can substitute their own simple patterns and perform the class version.
2	I can hear, read and respond to a range of rhymes and explore the way they are created by the way the text is laid out on the page. I can use a simple model from reading as a frame for writing.	Create people out of play dough as a starting point and stimulus for the poetry to be studied. Read and analyse *Playdough people* by Tony Mitton. Discuss what their dough people are like – record useful ideas and vocabulary for follow up work. List body parts and play with the words to find useful rhymes. Model writing new verses to add to the original poem with input from the children. Display the children's people along with a word-processed version of the poem with its new verses.	Children can explore how sounds, words and phrases are used and sequenced to produce poems and rhymes. Children can use rhymes as models for their own writing.
3	I can hear, read and respond to simple patterned stories. I can create silly couplets based on rhyme.	Read and share stories written in rhyme. Predict the rhymes and pick out rhyming pairs. Make lists of animals and create simple silly rhyming couplets.	Children can respond to simple patterned stories, identifying the patterned forms and use of rhyme. Children can create their own rhyming couplets using playful language choices.
4	I can hear, read and respond to a simple patterned story. I can identify the way words have been used and sequenced and laid out on the page. I can learn new vocabulary and use rhyming dictionaries to extend own vocabulary. I can use the model from reading as a frame for writing.	Discuss favourite book characters. Read *Fantastic Daisy Artichoke* by Quentin Blake. Analyse and identify rhymes. Discuss vocabulary. Group word cards by spelling. Matching exercise in groups. Use story as model for class book. List rhyming words and spell. Write up and illustrate class version.	Children can hear, read and respond to a story written in rhyme. Children can use this story as a framework for their own writing. Children can develop their vocabulary using rhyming dictionaries.

Provide copies of the objectives for the children.

DAY 1 ■ When I was one...

Key features	Stages	Additional opportunities
Enquiry: exploring patterns	**Introduction** Begin by asking children if they know any rhymes or poems about numbers (such as 'Five Little Ducks', 'Five Currant Buns', 'Ten Green Bottles' 'Ten in the bed'). Explain that you are going to learn a rhyme about a pirate ship and create a class version. **Speaking and listening** Teach the class *The pirate ship song* from the CD-ROM with associated actions. Sing and perform until everyone is confident with the words and actions. Ask what happened when they were two years old. Take the suggestion and insert it into the song. **Independent work** Encourage the children to use phonic skills and knowledge to suggest, spell and write words that rhyme with the numbers one to ten using photocopiable page 179 'Number rhymes'. Give the children rhyming dictionaries if these are available. **Plenary** Come together and write up the children's suggestions on photocopiable page 179. Encourage the children to use phonic knowledge and skills to spell the words as you record them in the table. Explain that these suggestions will be used to write their own rhymes for the song during the next lesson.	**Phonics:** b*un*, s*un*, sh*oe*, bl*ue*, tr*ee*, kn*ee*, d*oor*, sh*ore*, al*ive*, d*ive*, st*icks*, fix, h*ea*ven, eleven, pl*ate*, g*ate*, f*ine*, p*ine*, hen, men **HFW:** numbers one to ten **Support:** work in small groups with an adult **Extend:** work independently

DAY 2 ■ When I was two...

Key features	Stages	Additional opportunities
Communication: communicating through carefully chosen words	**Introduction** Sing *The pirate ship song* with actions! **Speaking and listening** Draw ten empty thought bubbles on the board. Invite children to come up and write the words for the numbers one to ten in each of the thought bubbles. Draw lines out from the thought bubbles and invite children to come up and write rhyming words for each number. Leave these displayed for children to use during independent work. **Independent work** Invite the children to use the rhyming words to create silly rhyming couplets for each of the numbers one to ten. **Plenary** Share the children's work and choose which rhyme the class likes best for the class version of the song.	**HFW:** numbers one to ten **Support:** work with an adult to make up all ten rhymes then choose their favourite to write up and illustrate on photocopiable page 180 'The pirate ship song' **Extend:** attempt all ten rhymes

DAY 3 ■ When I was three...

Key features	Stages	Additional opportunities
	Introduction Recap the class version of the song with the teacher scribing on the board.	**HFW:** numbers one to ten, when, I, was
	Speaking and listening Practise singing with the actions and celebrate the completion of the work!	
	Independent work Find a pirate ship template and ask the children to use their best handwriting to publish the poem. Allocate a verse to each child to write up in neat. They may like to colour the ship. Invite some children to use the computer to type up the verses onto the template.	
Evaluation: recording compositions as a vehicle for review	**Plenary** Mount the work in a folder or display it on the wall. Video or record the class performing the rhyme and play back to allow review and comment.	

Guided reading

Read a variety of poems and rhymes which contain numbers. Invite children to identify the numbers one to ten and locate the words that the poem uses to rhyme with them. Record them in vocabulary books or on white boards.

Assessment

On Day 2 explain that you will be marking the work sheets the children complete against agreed criteria. These criteria may be different for individual children but could include, choice of vocabulary and inventiveness of rhyme; use of phonic skills to spell new words, standard of handwriting.

Refer back to the learning outcomes on page 171.

Further work

Think of other rhymes such as 'One, Two, Buckle my shoe...' where you could substitute your own rhyming couplets. Create a display of poems and rhymes with numbers in. Display the numbers around the class to reinforce spelling of these high frequency words. Try rhyming with numbers to 20!

DAY 1 ☐ Playdough people - Tony Mitton

Key features	Stages	Additional opportunities
	Introduction Demonstrate how to model a person out of play dough, talking about the features and clothes you are adding. Give children a set time to make their own person. Explain that they will be used to help with the Literacy lesson later on.	**Phonics:** *fat, hat, faces, laces, legs, eggs, ball, all* **HFW:** are, and, some, a, have, with, like, up, in, aren't, at, all
	Speaking and listening Display *The Playdough people* in front of the class. Read the poem from the CD-ROM and ask: Do the descriptions sound like their own play dough people? What descriptions does the poet use? What do they notice about each verse? (first line repeated, second and fourth line rhyme). Identify the pairs of rhyming words, add to these lists.	
Communication: working collaboratively	**Independent work** In groups list other body parts and clothing. Use their people to give ideas and talk about what play dough people are like. Record suggestions for the plenary.	
	Plenary Write up sentences to describe each child's play dough person.	

DAY 2 ☐ Body parts for play dough people

Key features	Stages	Additional opportunities
	Introduction Re-read the poem *Playdough people* from the CD-ROM and recap what the children said about their own play dough people. Write up the list of body parts that have not been mentioned in the poem.	**Phonics:** *feet, seat* **HFW:** are, and, with, some, a, have, like, up, in, aren't, at, all
Enquiry: exploring patterns created by words	**Speaking and listening** Explain that you are going to write additional verses with the help of the class. Find useful rhyming words for the body parts mentioned (for example thumbs/tums, feet/neat/treat/seat/eat, knees/please/squeeze). Record these on the board. Recap the structure of each verse and model writing verses.	
Communication: discussing the language of poetry	**Independent work** Children write up the verse and illustrate it with a drawing of their own play dough person.	
	Plenary Recite the poem together following the displayed text.	

Guided reading
Read other poems and rhymes about people. Identify the way they are created by the way the text is laid out. Find rhyming couplets.

Assessment
Observe and record the contributions made by children during Speaking and listening against defined criteria - exploration of the text, ability to suggest rhyming words and so on. Refer back to the learning outcomes on page 171.

Further work
Make a collection of people poems to share during guided reading and independent reading time. Link with work on Ourselves.

DAY 1 ■ Patterned stories

Key features	Stages	Additional opportunities
Enquiry: exploring patterns created by words	### Introduction This Phase will move children on to looking at patterned stories with rhymes before using a patterned story in Phase 4 as a model for their own writing. Ask children if they know of any stories, particularly picture books which have a clear pattern or rhyme. Julia Donaldson's books such as *The Smartest Giant in Town*, *The Gruffalo* and *The Snail and the Whale* are all good examples.	**Phonics:** *dog, log, bog, cat, mat, sat, goat, boat, float* **HFW:** this, is, the, that
	### Speaking and listening Read and share *The Smartest Giant in Town*. List the animals which appear in the story and discuss what happened to them. List the rhymes.	
	### Independent work Invite children to choose an animal and write a silly, short rhyming couplets as follows: This is the _____ That_____ They can then illustrate their work.	**Support:** work in groups with an adult
	### Plenary Share the rhymes and highlight the rhymes used.	

Guided reading
Share other stories with patterns. Discuss how the text has been laid out, the nature of the pattern, (repeated lines, rhyming lines). Discuss preferences and reasons for expressed choices.

Assessment
Mark individual rhyming couplets against agreed criteria including the spelling of High Frequency Words, the choice of words and application of phonic skills to spell rhyming couplets. Refer back to the learning outcomes on page 171.

Further work
Word process pairs of rhyming words from the stories you have read. Laminate and make into cards for the children to play matching games with. Place the cards face down, take turns to turn over two cards. If the cards rhyme the child wins that pair. If they don't rhyme, the cards are replaced face down in their exact position ready for the next player to have a go.

DAY 1 ■ Daisy Artichoke – Quentin Blake

Key features	Stages	Additional opportunities
Enquiry: hearing, reading and responding to rhymes	### Introduction Discuss children's favourite characters from books and films, using pictures as a stimulus. What do they like about each character? What makes this character special or different? Do they have any special possessions or pets or wear particular clothes? Explain that you are going to share a patterned story which simply describes the character of a special lady called Daisy Artichoke. Read the story of *Fantastic Daisy Artichoke* or the poem from the CD-ROM. ### Speaking and listening Ask the children to listen carefully to the book and pick out all the things that make Daisy Artichoke who she is. They should listen too for rhyming words on each page. Read the book to the children all the way through, then again, stopping to look at the pictures and explaining vocabulary such as *stove, stoke, raven, soak.* ### Independent work Create a phonics sorting game, similar to the interactive assessment activity on the CD-ROM. Group cards according to how the long vowel sound is made. Children can then play a pairs matching a game with the cards. Place all the cards face down. Invite the children to take it in turns to turn over two cards – a pair is won if the long vowel sound is made in the same way on both cards. ### Plenary Carry out the game with the teacher against the class, using enlarged cards, encouraging the children to complete each line with an appropriate word.	**Phonics:** Artichoke, spoke, stroke, woke, broke, smoke, stoke, joke, soak, croak, cloak, oak, folk **HFW:** we, the, that, her, like, to, with, its, always, in, which, of, it, when, she, a, isn't, other **Support:** choose one card, highlight the letters making the *o* sound and invite children to find a similar one

DAY 2 ■ Class character book

Key features	Stages	Additional opportunities
	### Introduction Share the book, *Fantastic Daisy Artichoke* again. Ask children what they liked best about her eccentric character. Recap the 13 rhyming words which appeared in the book. Explain that as a class you are going to use Daisy Artichoke as a model for the class to write their own character book which uses a patterned rhyme.	**Phonics:** Artichoke, spoke, stroke, woke, broke, smoke, stoke, joke, soak, croak, cloak, oak, folk **HFW:** we, the, that, her, like, to, with, its, always, in, which, of, it, when, she, a, isn't, other
Enquiry: exploring patterns created by words **Communication:** discussing the language of poetry	### Speaking and listening Suggest a made up name with five syllables such as Betty Bittersweet or Charlie Coffeecake. Invite the children to think of words which rhyme with the chosen name. Pick a name which has plenty of useful rhyming words – for example: *feet, heat, seat, wheat, cheat, meet, meat* all rhyme with Betty Bittersweet. Record the children's suggestions. ### Independent work In groups with an adult assistant, encourage the children to play with the words to come up with possible lines for the class book. Remind children how each line was structured in *Fantastic Daisy Artichoke* and use this as a model. For example: *Here's our friend Charlie Coffeecake, A better friend you'll never make!* Record the ideas and retain for later use. ### Plenary Share ideas and agree which the class likes.	**Support:** use the differentiated text *Betty Bittersweet* from the CD-ROM as a model

DAY 3 ■ Creating a character

Key features	Stages	Additional opportunities
	Introduction Look at the pictures in *Fantastic Daisy Artichoke* and ask the children what they can remember about her. Remind the children of their own character's name, and explain that you are going to create your character today by putting together all the individual ideas.	**Phonics:** long vowel phonemes which rhyme
Enquiry: exploring patterns created by words	**Speaking and listening** Spread out all the individual lines or ideas that children came up with previously and model the creation of the new character-based patterned story. The differentiated text from the CD-ROM provides a completed alternative for Betty Bittersweet. Encourage the children to be as involved as possible with all aspects of the procedure. Demonstrate how their ideas can be used and played with to create effective rhymes. Create the poem using the computer to demonstrate that ideas can be easily changed if they do not work the first time.	**Support:** Children can complete the interactive activity 'Betty Bittersweet' from the CD-ROM
	Independent work Once the patterned story has been created, print out and cut up each line which lends itself to illustration. Assign pairs a line each to illustrate. Look at Quentin Blake's illustrative style. Explain that you would like them to plan their drawings which will be outlined in pencil prior to painting with watercolour. Meanwhile, pairs can take turns to use the keyboard to type up their line of the poem.	
	Plenary Re-read the class poem.	

DAY 4 ■ Betty Bittersweet's complete!

Key features	Stages	Additional opportunities
	Introduction Explain that the objective of the final session is to complete the publication of the illustrated, class patterned story and to celebrate the work by reciting it. The children will also have a chance to express views about the process and the completed work.	**Phonics:** long vowel sounds which rhyme
	Independent work Children complete their illustrations – ensuring that the pictures reflect the words. Allow them to paint or fill the illustrations with other suitable media, demonstrating the method. As they complete this, each child should use their best handwriting to write up their line to accompany the poem.	
Communication: communicating outcomes orally	**Plenary** Ask the children to bring their work together and organise it in the correct order. Recite the poem and invite the children to comment on what they liked about their poem, what they found difficult and so on. Mount the work in a topic book and allow it to be read by other classes alongside *Fantastic Daisy Artichoke*.	

Guided reading

Read *Fantastic Daisy Artichoke* together. Discuss the text and how it is laid out on the pages. Talk about the importance of the illustrations and the use of additional text aside from the main text (speech bubbles)

Read the class book and express views.

Assessment

Make observations during the modelling of the class story.

To assess the application of phonics ask the children to use the assessment activity 'Phonics sorting game' from the CD-ROM.

Refer back to the learning outcomes on page 171.

Further work

Using the rhyming words from the class patterned story, create your own long vowel sound matching game by typing up the words, printing out and cutting up. Children can then sort them into groups according to spelling.

Do this for other lists of rhyming words and use the words to create rhyming couplets.

Number rhymes

■ Write words that rhyme with each number in the boxes.

Number	Rhyming words			
One	bun	sun		
Two				
Three				
Four				
Five				
Six				
Seven				
Eight				
Nine				
Ten				

Name —————————————————— **Date** ——————————————

The pirate ship song

When I was ——————————————————

I ————————————————————————

————————————————————————

By ——————————————————————

■ 100 LITERACY FRAMEWORK LESSONS YEAR 1

POETRY
UNIT 3 Poems on a theme

Speak and listen for a range of purposes on paper and on screen

Strand 1 Speaking
■ Interpret a text by reading aloud with some variety in pace and emphasis.
Strand 2 Listening and responding
■ Listen with sustained concentration, building new stores of words in different contexts.
Strand 3 Group discussion and interaction
■ Ask and answer questions, make relevant contributions, offer suggestions and take turns.
■ Explain their views to others in a small group, decide how to report the group's views to the class.

Read for a range of purposes on paper and on screen

Strand 5 Word recognition: knowledge and skills
■ Recognise and use alternative ways of pronouncing and spelling the graphemes already taught.
■ Identify the constituent parts of two-syllable and three-syllable words to support the application of phonic knowledge and skills.
■ Recognise automatically an increasing number of familiar high frequency words.
■ Apply phonic knowledge and skills as the prime approach to reading and spelling unfamiliar words that are not completely decodable.
■ Read more challenging texts which can be decoded using their acquired phonic knowledge and skills, along with automatic recognition of high frequency words.
■ Read and spell phonically decodable two-syllable and three-syllable words.
Strand 6 Understanding and interpreting texts
■ Spell new words using phonics as the prime approach
■ Segment sounds into their constituent phonemes in order to spell them correctly.
■ Recognise and use alternative ways of spelling the graphemes already taught.
■ Use knowledge of common inflections in spelling, such as plurals, -ly, -er.
■ Read and spell phonically decodable two-syllable and three-syllable words.
Strand 7 Engaging and responding to texts
■ Explain the effect of patterns of language and repeated words and phrases.
Strand 8 Creating and shaping texts
■ Visualise and comment on events, characters and ideas, making imaginative links to their own experiences.

Write for a range of purposes on paper and on screen

Strand 9 Text structure and organisation
■ Find and use new and interesting words and phrases, including story language.
■ Create short simple texts on paper and on screen that combine words with images (and sounds).
Strand 12 Presentation
■ Write most letters, correctly formed and orientated, using a comfortable and efficient pencil grip.
■ Write with spaces between words accurately.

▶

UNIT 3 ◄ Poems on a theme *continued*

Progression in poetry

In this year, children are moving towards:
■ Discussing own response and what the poem is about; talking about favourite words or parts of the poem; noticing the poem's pattern.
■ Performing in unison following the rhythm and keeping time.
■ Observing details of first hand experiences using the senses to describe.

Key aspects of learning covered in this Unit

Enquiry
Children will listen to poems, look at pictures, explore props to help them consider how they feel and view the seaside.

Reasoning
Children will explain their preferences for different poems. They will explain the words and phrases they chose to describe different aspects of the seaside.

Evaluation
Children will discuss success criteria for describing the seaside, give feedback to others and judge the effectiveness of their word choices.

Empathy and self-awareness
Children will read and hear about the experiences of others at the seaside and compare it to their own.

Communication
They will begin to develop their ability to discuss the language of poetry and to communicate their own experiences and observations through carefully chosen words. They will work collaboratively in pairs or groups and as a class. They will communicate outcomes orally and in writing and using ICT.

Prior learning

Before starting this Unit check that the children can:
■ Listen to poems being read and talk about likes and dislikes.
■ Join in with class rhymes and poems. Copy actions.
■ Enjoy making up funny sentences and playing with words.
■ Look carefully at experiences and choose words to describe.
■ Make word collections.
If they need further support refer to a prior Unit or to the Foundation Stage.

Resources

Phase 1: Seaside props; *Over my toes* by Michael Rosen ❧; Silky material; *Sing a song of seasons* by Celia Warren ❧
Phase 2: *On the beach* by Michael Rosen ❧
Phase 3: *Song of the seaside* by Celia Warren ❧; Photocopiable page 191 'Seaside cards'; Photocopiable page 192 'Songs of the seaside'
Phase 4: *Footprints on the beach* by John Foster ❧; Assessment activity 'Seaside poems' ❧

Cross-curricular opportunities

History (seaside holidays in the past)

UNIT 3 ■ Teaching sequence

Phase	Children's objectives	Summary of activities	Learning outcomes
1	I can listen and respond to poems about the seaside. I can listen to the views of others. I can offer opinions about my favourite parts or words. I can make word collections based on my own experiences and feelings.	Read *Over my toes* by Michael Rosen and study use of words and structure. Use shells to 'listen' to the sea. Think of words to describe the sea from their own experiences. Read and discuss *Sing a song of seasons*. Create powerful phrases to describe aspects of the seaside and add to word collection. Paint two large background scenes – the seaside in summer and the seaside in winter – for a collage. Paint a seaside feature for the collage. Word-process phrases to describe each feature and add to collage.	Children can communicate their own experiences in words. Children can listen to poems and select their favourite parts. Children can listen respectfully to the views of others. Children can suggest powerful words linked to the senses to describe the seaside.
2	I can use free verse. I can notice patterns in a poem and use them as a model for my own writing.	Use the collage to select effective phrases to create free verse. Perform the class poem. Read *On the beach* by Michael Rosen and identify the structure. Think of seaside words and rhymes for these words. Create more similar verses.	Children can create a powerful phrase using carefully chosen vocabulary to contribute to a class free verse. Children can identify pattern in a poem. Children can use simple structures as a coat hanger for their own ideas.
3	I can study the pattern of a simple poem and use it as a model for my own writing.	Read *Song of the seaside* by Celia Warren. Work in pairs to write own version. Publish the poem and perform the poem with props.	Children can perform poems with actions and props.
4	I can compare similarities and differences between poems and express opinions about preferences.	Read *Footprints on the beach* by John Foster and discuss the structure of the poem. Paint and cut out footprints and use these to write up their verse. Re-read all the poems studied in Unit 3. Discuss preferences and reasons. Carry out a poll.	Children can use a starting point to add on their own ideas. Children can make comparisons between different poems. Children can select their favourite poems and give reasons for their choices.

Provide copies of the objectives for the children.

DAY 1 ▪ Over my toes – Michael Rosen

Key features	Stages	Additional opportunities
Empathy and self-awareness: experiences of the seaside	**Introduction** Introduce the seaside theme of the Unit using props. Explain the objectives clearly, as formative assessment will be carried out at the end of each Phase. Discuss seaside experiences encouraging turn taking. Ask the children to sit children in two rows with their shoes and socks off and close their eyes. Shake a piece of silky material over their feet while reading *Over my toes* from the CD-ROM. Ask the children how the words helped them to feel the sea. **Speaking and listening** Display *Over my toes*. Point while children count the number of words in the poem (43). Use different colours to highlight words which are repeated. Now count how many *different* words are in the poem (13). Ask: *Why has the poet repeated words?* (To create the sound of the sea and the ebb and flow of the tide.) *What letter and clusters do lots of the words begin and end with?* **Independent work** Put the children in groups with an adult scribe, large piece of paper and a large shell for each group. Explain that people say that the sea can be heard if you put a shell to your ear. Think of words and phrases to describe the smell, feel, and sound of the sea both on sunny days and when the weather is bad. Encourage expansion of ideas – sandy shore, angry waves, foaming waters. **Plenary** Share the ideas and give positive feedback to each other.	**Phonics:** *sl*ap, *sl*ip, *sl*ide, wa*sh* **HFW:** over, my, the, see, goes

DAY 2 ▪ Sing a song of seasons

Key features	Stages	Additional opportunities
Communication: discussing the language of poetry	**Introduction** Recite the nursery rhyme 'Sing a Song of Sixpence' as a class. Display and read *Sing a song of seasons* from the CD-ROM. Ask the children to comment on how the poet has used the nursery rhyme as a frame for a seaside poem. Identify the rhymes and briefly identify phonics opportunities. Compare the verses – one describes the sea in summer, one the sea in winter. **Independent work** Split the class into two groups with an adult leading each group. On large pieces of paper, one group will paint a seaside background (just sea, sand and sky) in winter and the other a seaside background in summer. While painting, the adult leads a discussion about what they might see, hear, smell, feel on the beach in their chosen season. **Plenary** Record the suggestions alongside those suggested on Day 1, to create a bank of powerful words and phrases about the seaside.	**Phonics:** *s*and, *h*and, *s*aves, *w*aves, *cr*y, *dr*y, *p*ours, *r*oars **HFW:** a, of, and, in, my, some, are, the, not, so, we, them, when, it

DAY 3 ■ Seaside scenes

Key features	Stages	Additional opportunities
Communication: communicating their experiences through carefully chosen words	### Introduction Explain that today the class is going to build a collage of pictures and words onto the seaside backgrounds. Each child will create (in a medium such as paint or pastel) an image that will be cut out and stuck onto the background. Provide children with an appropriate-sized paper and tell them that you would like them to fill the paper. The children's next task will be to word process a phrase to describe their image. These will be printed, cut up and stuck onto the collage. Using the word and phrase bank for summer and winter seaside scenes collected on Days 1 and 2, invite the children to choose what they would like to contribute to the collage. ### Independent work Ask the children to create their image and take turns to use the keyboard to word process the accompanying description. ### Plenary The work is added to the backgrounds to create two contrasting seaside scenes. Children express opinions about which descriptions they particularly like and why.	

Guided reading
Invite the children to look through school poetry anthologies to locate other seaside poems. Read and compare them with those studied so far.

Assessment
At the beginning of Phase 1 explain the objectives and what the children are working towards. If they achieve their objectives, award Achievement Stickers stating what they have achieved: *I can listen carefully to poems and identify patterns* and *I can choose words carefully to describe the seaside.* For children who need to work further to achieve these objectives, award Target Stickers, to be worked on during the next Unit: *My target is to listen carefully to poems so that I can understand how they have been written* and *My target is to think carefully about the words I choose for my poems.*
Refer back to the learning outcomes on page 183.

Further work
Use other nursery rhymes as a framework for creating poems about the sea. A simple example is *Here We Go Round the Mulberry Bush.* It lends itself well to two versions – one for the summer and one for the winter.

DAY 1 ■ Free verse

Key features	Stages	Additional opportunities
Communication: choosing words carefully	### Introduction Explain that poems are essentially paintings with words which create pictures in the reader's mind. Highlight that poems do not have to rhyme but that it is important to carefully choose words that are powerful and expressive and that use all the senses. Today they are going to take the most powerful images and phrases from their actual painting and create a class free verse about the seaside which will create an image of the sea in the reader's mind.	
Evaluation: discussing the effectiveness of their word choices	### Independent work Split into two groups: winter and summer seaside. Model how to pull phrases from the collage, adapt them, use dictionaries and create a class verse. Involve the children's suggestions and help them to consider their choices carefully. Write the words on a large sheet of paper. Demonstrate how to edit. ### Plenary Each group reports their verse. Display this and as a class read and review each verse.	

DAY 2 ■ On the beach – Michael Rosen

Key features	Stages	Additional opportunities
Communication: choosing words carefully	### Introduction As a contrast to the free verse, *On the beach* by Michael Rosen provides an example of a nonsense poem about the seaside where the use of rhyme creates the nonsense. Display and read the poem from the CD-ROM. Invite children to comment on the structure. Line 1 states who the poem is about. Line 2 states where they are on the beach and lines 3 and 4 describe what is happening. Identify the rhymes in each verse and discuss why it is nonsense. Think of seaside words (such as crab, pool, spade) and list any useful words which rhyme with them.	**Phonics:** *sand, hand, rocks, socks, sea, me, chair, bear* **HFW:** there, a, over, and, he, is, in, the, at, now, for, his, her, she, me, see, girl, on
	### Independent work The poem details the activities of a man, woman, boy and girl on the beach. In groups, think about what creatures may be on the beach (crab, seagull, shell, donkey, fish). Brainstorm where these creatures may be (a pool, the sky, on the beach, in the sea). Suggest silly things the creatures could be. ### Plenary Use the ideas to create verses for your own poem about the beach.	**Support:** provide non-fiction books with plenty of illustrations as visual support

Guided reading

Share a selection of nonsense poems by Edward Lear with groups during guided reading.

Assessment

For those children who achieve the Phase objectives, award Achievement Statement stickers: *I can listen carefully to identify how a poem has been written* and *I can choose powerful words to describe the seaside*. Give Target Statements to those not meeting the objectives, to be worked towards during the next Phase: *My target is to choose my own powerful words to write a seaside poem*.

Refer back to the learning outcomes on page 183.

Further work

Read other Michael Rosen poems and discuss his style of writing. Ask: *Are all his poems light hearted? Does he always use rhyme? Which poems do they like best and why?*

Use a visual stimulus with the children with Target Statements to encourage the use of powerful descriptive words.

DAY 1 ▪ Song of the seaside

Key features	Stages	Additional opportunities
Communication: discussing the language of poetry	**Introduction** Think of rhymes which use numbers ('One, Two, Buckle my shoe', 'This old man, he played one'). Display and read *Song of the seaside* from the CD-ROM. Study the form of the poem, annotating the text where appropriate. Hand out the prompt cards from photocopiable page 191 'Seaside cards' and use them to recite the poem as a class. Highlight the words which are not on the prompt cards and read these together. Rehearse until the poem has pace and rhythm.	**Phonics:** sp*a*de, m*a*de, t*o*wel, h*o*wl, sky, fly **HFW:** for, a, the, that, me, we, like, to, numbers one to nine
	Speaking and listening Ask the children to think of new words to add to the seaside word list from Phase 2, then to find words which rhyme with the new words.	
	Independent work Ask the children to use the word lists to create their own 'Song of the seaside'.	**Support:** work in a group with an adult
Evaluation: giving feedback	**Plenary** Invite the children to share their work and comment on each other's ideas.	

DAY 2 ▪ Seaside performance

Key features	Stages	Additional opportunities
	Introduction Recite *Song of the seaside* again as a class. Invite the children to perform their own versions for the class.	**HFW:** for, a, the, numbers one to nine
	Independent work Ask the children to work independently to write up their poems for display. Some children may like to use photocopiable page 192 'Song of the seaside' to support their writing. Children may use ICT to source images to support their poems or illustrate them around the border.	**Support:** use photocopiable page 192 to present their poem
Evaluation: giving feedback	**Plenary** Allow children to share their work and give each other positive feedback.	

Guided reading
Locate a selection of poems and rhymes which include numbers to read, share and compare.

Assessment
At the end of Phase 3, the Achievement Statement stickers are: *I can find pairs of rhyming words* and *I can write my own seaside poem.*
For those children who need to work further to achieve these objectives, the Target Statements are: *My target is to find pairs of rhyming words* and *My target is to write my own seaside poem.*
Refer back to the learning outcomes on page 183.

Further work
For those children awarded Target Statements, read simple poems with rhyming couplets and encourage the children to identify the pairs of rhyming words.

DAY 1 ■ Footprints on the beach – John Foster

Key features	Stages	Additional opportunities
Communication: discussing the language of poetry	**Introduction** Display and read the poem *Footprints on the beach* from the CD-ROM. Ask: *Which verse is repeated?* (First.) *What is the first word of the other verses?* (The name of the print). *How is each verse written?* (As a rhyming couplet.) Identify the rhymes. **Independent work** Split the class into two groups. Set up a tray of wet sand with sticks or wooden spoons to use as writing implements. Invite the children to use the trays for writing. They may also like to create footprints. Ask the second group to create new verses for the poem using first lines provided by you. Ensure that the lines provide easy rhyming opportunities. For example: *Towel prints show where mum was snoring... Small footprints show where toddlers play...* Groups should then swap activities. **Plenary** Discuss the rhymes that originated from the group work.	**Phonics:** show, go, bound, around, tracks, backs, stand, sand, tread, bread, dash, splash **HFW:** the, who, comes, where, they, go, upon, dog, for, of, and **Support:** scribe for the children **Extend:** create own first lines

DAY 2 ■ Footprint fun

Key features	Stages	Additional opportunities
	Introduction Ask the class to suggest what children like to do on the beach and how their footprints would reflect their activity. Explain that children will use these ideas to write their own free verse about what they would like to do on the beach and what their footprints show.	**HFW:** my, where, I
Communication: communicating through carefully chosen words	**Independent work** Invite the children to take turns to create two footprints using yellow paint. While waiting to paint, ask the children to draft how they wish to complete the following: *My footprints show where I...* The poem should not be restricted by rhyme but should demonstrate carefully chosen words to create an image in the reader's mind of the child on the beach. Children should be encouraged to apply their phonic knowledge to spell and write the words they have chosen in draft format.	**Support:** work with an adult
Evaluation: giving feedback	**Plenary** Encourage the children to read out their poems and comment constructively on each other's work.	

DAY 3 ■ The seaside

Key features	Stages	Additional opportunities

Communication: discussing the language of poetry

Introduction

Use this final lesson to draw together all the poems on the theme of the seaside. Re-read the five poems studied as well as any others used to supplement these. Bring together all the children's work completed during the Phase: the seaside collage, 'The sea' (free verse), 'On the beach', 'Song of the seaside' and 'Footprints'. Review the process of writing poetry – thinking of words, choosing words selectively, making up rhymes, creating nonsense verse, writing free verse, creating images to support writing. Discuss the parts children enjoyed the most, what they found difficult and what they think they did well.

Independent work

Ask the children to work individually or in small groups to complete the assessment activity 'Seaside poems'.

Plenary

Come together and invite the children to share their opinions. They can then carry out a vote to see which poem the class liked best. Present the results of the vote as a bar chart and write a statement expressing the results.

Guided reading

Create a poetry corner where all the poems studied and the work completed can be displayed along with seaside props. Put beanbags or comfy chairs to make the corner inviting. Add to this poetry anthologies which contain seaside poems. Tape recorders with headphones and tapes of the children reading the poems may also be a feature of the corner. Carry out guided reading sessions in this area to encourage a love of poetry. Once the seaside theme has been completed, maintain the poetry corner and change the theme.

Assessment

At the end of the fourth Phase, the child Achievement Statements to be awarded are: *I can write a rhyming couplet, I can create my own free verse* and *I can tell the class what I think about the poems I have read.* The Target Statement for this Phase is more general and can be worked towards during guided reading sessions: *My target is to be able to tell my teacher my thoughts about what I read.*
Refer back to the learning outcomes on page 183.

Further work

Hang mobiles above the poetry corner – these could be a sunshine, clouds, kites, seagulls and windsurfers. On the mobile write the names of poems and ask the children to give the poems scores out of ten. They may also categorise the poem as funny, imaginative, serious, nonsense and so on.

Seaside cards

✂ ■ Cut out the cards to use as props.

1 one	2 two	3 three	4 four	5 five	6 six
7 seven	8 eight	9 nine	bucket	spade	castle
deckchair	towel	crab	sunshine	sky	kite

Illustrations © Nova Developments.

■ SCHOLASTIC **PHOTOCOPIABLE**
www.scholastic.co.uk

Name _____   Date _____

Song of the seaside

One for _____

Two for _____

Three for _____

_____

Four for _____

Five for _____

Six for _____

_____

Seven for _____

Eight for _____

Nine for _____

_____

■ 100 LITERACY FRAMEWORK LESSONS YEAR 1

PHOTOCOPIABLE   ■SCHOLASTIC
www.scholastic.co.uk